LET'S STUDY
COLOSSIANS
& PHILEMON

Series Editor: SINCLAIR B. FERGUSON

Let's Study

COLOSSIANS
& PHILEMON

Mark G. Johnston

THE BANNER OF TRUTH TRUST

THE BANNER OF TRUTH TRUST
3 Murrayfield Road, Edinburgh EH12 6EL, UK
P.O. Box 621, Carlisle, PA 17013, USA

*

© Mark G. Johnston 2013

ISBN:
Print: 978 1 84871 239 3
Kindle: 978 1 84871 240 9
EPUB: 978 1 84871 241 6

*

Typeset in 11/12.5pt Ehrhardt MT at the
Banner of Truth Trust, Edinburgh

Printed in the U.S.A. by
Versa Press, Inc.,
East Peoria, IL

FOR
COLLIER
AND
IN LOVING MEMORY
OF
BEVERLEE

Contents

LET'S STUDY COLOSSIANS & PHILEMON

Publisher's Preface

*L*et's *Study Colossians & Philemon* is part of a series of books which explain and apply the message of Scripture. The series is designed to meet a specific and important need in the church. While not technical commentaries, the volumes comment on the text of a biblical book; and, without being merely lists of practical applications, they are concerned with the ways in which the teaching of Scripture can affect and transform our lives today. Understanding the Bible's message and applying its teaching are the aims.

Like other volumes in the series, *Let's Study Colossians & Philemon* seeks to combine explanation and application. Its concern is to be helpful to ordinary Christian people by encouraging them to understand the message of the Bible and apply it to their own lives. The reader in view is not the person who is interested in all the detailed questions which fascinate the scholar, although behind the writing of each study lies an appreciation for careful and detailed scholarship. The aim is exposition of Scripture written in the language of a friend, seated alongside you with an open Bible.

Let's Study Colossians & Philemon is designed to be used in various contexts. It can be used simply as an aid for individual Bible study. Some may find it helpful to use in their devotions with husband or wife, or to read in the context of the whole family.

In order to make these studies more useful, not only for individual use but also for group study in Sunday School classes and home, church, or college, study guide material will be found on pages 157-178. Sometimes we come away frustrated rather than helped by group discussions. Frequently that is because we have been encouraged to discuss a passage of Scripture which we do not understand very well in the first place. Understanding must always be the foundation for enriching discussion and for thoughtful, practical application. Thus, in addition to the exposition of the letters, the additional material provides questions to encourage personal thought and study, or to be used as discussion starters. The Group Study Guide divides the material into fourteen sections and provides direction for leading and participating in group study and discussion.

Foreword

Bible study is not a luxury, it is a necessity. From the earliest time in the history of the church, the Scriptures have been at the very heart of the spiritual life and well-being of God's people.

When they were preparing to enter the Promised Land, Moses told the Israelites that God's Word was to be in their hearts as much as in their heads and it was to suffuse every aspect of their life as families and as a community (*Deut.* 6:4-9). The Psalms, which in so many ways reflect the heartbeat of the church through all ages, begin with a focus on meditating on God's teaching day and night (*Psa.* 1:1); the longest psalm in the collection is an extended reflection on how Scripture shapes the life of faith. When God's people lost their way spiritually on a monumental scale and ended up in exile, it was a return to the Word under Ezra and Nehemiah that brought them back to where they were meant to be with God (*Neh.* 8:1-8).

Many centuries later in New Testament times the Apostle Peter captured it well when he said that it is by the Word that people are brought into a new and living relationship with God, and it is through that same Word that they are nourished in their faith and grow to know and love God more (*1 Pet.* 1:22-2:2). Bible study matters.

There are, of course, many different ways we can study the Bible and, perhaps surprisingly, what we often call 'Bible Study' – when people get together as a group to discuss a verse or a passage – is not the most obvious. That kind of approach to exploring the message of the Bible is a relatively recent development in the history of the church – not least because it is only in relatively recent times that the ability to read has become so widespread.

In past centuries people 'studied' the Bible by hearing it read and having it explained to them by those who were the appointed teachers of the church. This is still a very important part of how we learn as Christians today. Some of the most important gifts Christ has given the church are, according to Paul, those 'pastor-teachers' who are able to instruct God's people and equip them for service (*Eph.* 4:11-13). In a very special way they are called to serve God and serve his people by becoming servants (ministers) of his Word. In that sense, some of the most important 'Bible Study' we can do is to simply sit under that Word as it is preached each Lord's Day in our churches.

That was certainly the normal way that people would be instructed in the Scriptures for the greater part of church history, but it was not the only way. People were also encouraged to memorise portions of the Bible – 'store it up in their heart' (*Psa.* 119:11) – and then meditate upon it. The whole idea of meditating, according to the Bible, is not some kind of religious mysticism but rather disciplined thinking about what a passage means and then reflecting on the ways it applies to our lives so that we begin to be shaped by its truth. In that sense, meditation has become something of a lost art for many Christians today, but one that urgently needs to be rediscovered.

The third main way in which we can do Bible Study is, as we have already hinted, by getting together in groups (preferably led by someone who has studied a passage more deeply) and learn together as we discuss what it says, what it means, and how it applies to our lives. Group studies like these provide a natural and non-threatening opportunity not only to articulate and sharpen our own understanding of particular parts of the Bible, but also to have the freedom to ask questions about the bits we do not understand. They also provide a useful entry point for people who want to find out about the Bible and the promise of salvation it contains.

All three of these approaches to Bible Study in many ways converge in the tool you happen to be holding in your hand: a book. Books on the Bible like this one have often been written by those who have been trained as Bible teachers and have served either in churches or Bible colleges in some capacity. (Indeed, what they end up writing in books like these is frequently a written version of what they have already taught in a classroom or preached from a pulpit.) The whole purpose of Bible commentaries like this one is to open up the message of the Bible by letting it speak for itself. The further value of Bible Study in book form is that we can use it for our own private study, or we can use it with others as we get together for discussion in groups.

I very much hope that, whether you choose to use this commentary on Colossians for private study or together with others, you will find it helpful as you dig more deeply into the teaching of this wonderful part of the New Testament Scriptures.

It is impossible to go through the exercise of writing any book without being deeply conscious of the many different people who have contributed to it in ways they could never imagine. For me, the impact of my wife and now grown up children has been enormous. The Bible comes to life in all kinds of ways in the crucible of home and family life. I am ever grateful for Fiona, Lindsay and Andrew, and for all they mean to me and the way they have shaped my life. The church family is another major factor in the way God shapes us as individuals. There is a very real sense in which Bible Study can never be a private and personal exercise, because we always end up studying Scripture in community – leaning upon the wisdom and insight of those who have gone before us as much as on those around us as we wrestle with the text. Much of the wrestling with the text of Colossians that has been distilled in this volume was done in Grove Chapel in Camberwell, South London in a series of sermons delivered there some years ago. I owe an enormous debt to that congregation for the way my years with them shaped and moulded me in the faith and in the ministry in all kinds of ways. I am also tremendously grateful to my current congregation, Proclamation Presbyterian Church in Bryn Mawr, Pennsylvania. Its Session and members have been extremely kind and supportive in granting a generous measure of study leave each year, part of which has enabled me to complete the work involved in writing this volume.

There is another friendship that has meant a great deal to me and my family over many years. It began through weekly jogging outings and a monthly Gourmet Club and led to our longstanding bond with Collier and Beverlee Kirkland. They knew what it was to live with suffering as an everyday part of their life – a suffering that would eventually lead to bereavement. But their faith, and joy through that suffering blessed us enormously and many others besides. This book is dedicated to Collier and to the fond memory of his much-loved wife, Beverlee.

MARK G. JOHNSTON
Proclamation Presbyterian Church
Bryn Mawr, Pennsylvania
December 2011

COLOSSIANS

Introduction to Colossians

We live in an age in which the idea of 'mass communication' has taken on an altogether new meaning. If the invention of the printing press heralded a new era that was to shape the course of history for the next 600 years, then it is hard to imagine the scale of the potential that is bound up with the age of electronic communication. 'Books' can now be accessed at the touch of a button in the middle of the Sahara! But there is a downside to it all. The sheer volume of material that is available and the novelty of so many ideas that are swirling around can make us lose our bearings in life in all kinds of ways. Nowhere is that more true than in our understanding of what it means to be a Christian and what is bound up with living the Christian life. All too often Christians and churches, as much as those who want to find out about the Christian faith, are shaped by the latest ideas about Christianity instead of the timeless truths of the Bible which form its true foundation.

Ironically this is not as new a problem as we might imagine. Even in Bible times the same problem surfaced again and again. In Jeremiah's day, when the Jews had been led astray through new teachings that claimed to come from God, but had not, the prophet had to call God's people back to 'the ancient paths' of God's truth revealed (*Jer.* 6:16). The same was true in Paul's day too. Much of his letter-writing was devoted to countering false teachings that were damaging the church on two fronts. The first, which emerged largely from those who professed to be Christians and had come from a Jewish background, was through a distortion of the message of the Old Testament Scriptures. The second was through the broader influences of the philosophies and religions of the Greek and Roman world in which the early church found itself. On both fronts his response was always the same: to draw people back to what God had revealed in his Word and ultimately to the way that revelation always finds its focus in Christ and the promise of salvation.

As we begin our studies in Paul's letter to the Colossians, we see both these strands of false teaching creeping into their church, and we see Paul responding to it, not merely by pointing afresh to God's revealed Word, but in a very striking way to God's Word as it finds its focus in Christ.

Before we start to look in detail at the actual text of the letter, it would be helpful for us to pause for a moment and fill in a few background details that will give us a better feel for the context into which its message came.

THE PLACE AND THE CULTURE

The city of Colossae was located in the Lycus Valley in the south-west region of what used to be known as Asia Minor, but is now modern-day Turkey. Because it lay on one of the great trade routes of the ancient world, it had once been a thriving centre of commerce, but for some two centuries prior to this letter being written it had fallen into decline. Its importance as a city was eclipsed by Laodicea and Hierapolis, two of its near neighbours.

The city is mentioned by a number of ancient historians including Herodotus, Xenophon and Strabo. The picture that we get from them is of a city that had become quite cosmopolitan in its heyday, the residue of which was still there at the time this letter was written.

A significant part of the residual influence of Colossae's past can be seen in the mix of religious influences in the region generally and this city in particular. The cult of Cybele flourished in this part of Asia Minor and produced a strange blend of ecstatic and ascetic practices. Other elements of Greek and Roman religions were present as well. However, the note by the Jewish historian Josephus, that Antiochus III brought some two thousand Jews from Babylon and Mesopotamia into this region during the early part of the second century B.C., adds another dimension to our understanding of the situation in which the Colossian church found itself. These historical details, especially as they relate to the religious *milieu* of the region, may well help to explain the rather unusual mixture of issues that were affecting the spiritual health of its people. In particular, the way that issues of Jewish ceremonialism and pagan practices seem to have surfaced at the same time in the church.

THE CHURCH IN COLOSSAE

The general background of the city and its culture – not least because by New Testament times Colossae had become something of a backwater – raises the question of how the gospel got there in the first place. There is no reason to think that Paul ever visited it in person. His priority on his missionary journeys was to head for the more influential centres of population of which Colossae was not one. However, there is good reason to believe that he was indirectly involved in seeing a church planted in this community.

The reference to 'Epaphras, who is one of you' (4:12) and the fact that it was this same man who brought the gospel to Colossae (1:7), clearly identify him as a key figure in any explanation of how the church came to be there. Add to this the fact that Paul has such a high regard for him as a co-worker and messenger of the gospel as well as the reference in Acts to the far-reaching impact of the apostle's three-year ministry in Ephesus (*Acts* 19:10) and we have good reason to believe that Epaphras came to faith through Paul's preaching in that city and then returned to his hometown to proclaim the same message to his fellow countrymen.

This helps to explain why Paul's message to the Colossians comes across with such warmth and pastoral concern, despite the fact he has never met them in person. His closeness to Epaphras gave him an intimate knowledge of all that God had been doing in the congregation with which his dear friend was so involved; so much so, that when things began to go wrong in that church, Paul was eager to write to the fellowship and address the issues it was facing.

THE COLOSSIAN PROBLEM

Most of Paul's letters were written in response to specific problems that came up in particular churches or groups of churches. It is normally fairly straightforward to identify what those problems were. However, in the case of Paul's letter to the Colossians, identifying the issues facing the church is not an easy task. In order to build up some kind of profile of what the issues were, we need to piece together a number of clues found in the text.

The clues fall into two main categories. On the one hand there are symptoms of unhealthy practices creeping into the life of the church. Some came from a Jewish background relating to food and drink laws, the observance of holy days and ceremonial practices (most notably circumcision). Other unhealthy practices arose out of a pagan background (with strong echoes of the ascetic and ecstatic elements of the cults that were common in that region): these included angel worship, secret knowledge, and the exaltation of human wisdom and traditions.

The other major set of clues that we find in the body of the letter is seen in the kind of things Paul majors on. The most obvious of these is his strong focus on the person and work of Christ. Whatever was going wrong in the church at Colossae, its most alarming symptom was a drift away from Jesus Christ as he is presented in the gospel.

Despite the complexities of trying to make sense of the Colossian church's problems, lessons can be drawn out from this letter that are applicable for every church. One such lesson is the sheer subtlety of the way false teachings can creep into faithful churches. Often it is only as a worrying accumulation of symptoms show themselves that we begin to wonder what really lies behind them. The individual symptoms may seem fairly innocuous in themselves, but when we stand back and see them altogether, alarm bells start to ring. But almost invariably the acid test of the spiritual health of a church is whether or not Christ is at its heart – not just in some vague and general sense, but Christ in all his glory as he is set before us in God's Word.

In that sense, even though the 'Colossian problem' is tied to a particular place in the world and a specific time in history, the issues bound up with it have surfaced again and again throughout the life of the church. So, being aware of what was happening there and then in the past has a lot to say to us in what we are facing here and now in the present.

THE DATE AND THE AUTHOR

Bible commentaries will almost always have a section in their intro-
ductions that raises the questions of authorship and date. Readers
who are either new to the Christian faith, or who are only beginning to study the Bible seriously may rightly wonder why such
questions need to be addressed – especially as the discussions that
surround them can often feel more than a little esoteric. Such questions neeed to be answered because there are many writings that
date from biblical times that look and feel as though they could
have a place in the Bible. The books included in the Apocrypha,
which were written during the four centuries before the coming of
Christ, are a prime example of this. However, when they are put
under close scrutiny it becomes clear that those books do not bear
the marks of having come ultimately from God; they are merely
the compositions of men who were writing about God.

As we approach this particular New Testament letter, the same
questions need to be asked, not least because in more recent times
Bible scholars have queried whether or not Colossians really was
written by Paul, even though Paul is named in its opening verse.
Their argument is that the secret knowledge and ecstatic experience issues that are addressed in the letter seem to be similar to
issues that confronted the church at a later period, during the second century A.D., in the cult of Gnosticism. If this was the main
issue that was affecting the church in Colossae, then the letter
could not have been written by Paul. And if that be the case, then
Colossians does not carry apostolic authority and so has no place in
the New Testament.

However, despite the challenges that have been raised by some
Bible scholars, there remains a very strong consensus that the kind
of issues that were emerging in Colossae were not as fully developed as those that troubled the church during the second century.
This fact along with other factors that relate to the style of writing and similarities with other letters written by Paul, support the
belief that this book does have apostolic credentials and therefore
does indeed have a place in Scripture.

The question of where and when the letter was written ties in
with this, in that Paul was in prison at the time of writing. Three
other letters, Philemon, Ephesians, and Philippians were also

written when the apostle was in prison, and Colossians carries some notable echoes of the kind of issues that are addressed in those other letters too. There has been some debate as to which of Paul's imprisonments is in view here, but most scholars believe it was the time mentioned at the end of the Acts of the Apostles, when Paul was under house arrest in Rome. This would date the letter to some time in or around A.D. 60.

COLOSSIANS FOR TODAY

Putting all these details together it appears that Paul was writing to a church that was still relatively young, but which was being destabilized by a mixture of influences from the Jewish and pagan cultures in which it found itself. His response was to bring the focus of God's people firmly back on to Jesus Christ – his person and work – to show that the fullness and sufficiency of God's great salvation are found in him, and in him alone.

As we begin to look more closely at what the apostle had to say to that church in its day, we quickly realize that this is nothing less than the Holy Spirit speaking to the church of our day as well.

I

More than Just a Greeting

Paul, an apostle of Christ Jesus by the will of God, and Timothy our brother, ² To the saints and faithful brothers in Christ at Colossae: Grace to you and peace from God our Father (Col. 1:1–2).

The art of letter-writing was well established in the Greek and Roman world of Paul's day and, as with every age and culture, it had its own respected protocols and conventions. Unlike the conventions of letter-writing in our own day (which are rapidly being replaced by those of email and texting), the person writing the letter would identify himself or herself at the start, before addressing the person or persons to whom they were writing. This in turn would normally lead in to a fairly standard salutation of 'Greetings!'

Paul, however, was no ordinary letter-writer and even though he wrote many letters in a private and personal capacity, there were thirteen occasions when he wrote self-consciously in a way that conveyed a great deal more. These are the letters of Paul that we find in the New Testament and in each of them, he writes with a deep awareness that he does so, not with his own authority, but with that of God himself. Colossians is one of those letters.

In that sense, as he greets the congregation at Colossae, he adapts the conventions of normal correspondence to serve a higher purpose: that of a communication from God himself. And just as there are no wasted words in any part of God's wider communication in Scripture, so here – even in the opening paragraph – every word is pressed into service as God through Paul addresses the needs of his church.

WORDS SPOKEN WITH AUTHORITY

People today have grown increasingly sceptical of those who make great promises, but who have no authority to honour them. Whether it be a cold-calling salesperson offering some financial product that seems too good to be true, or a letter saying we are one of a handful of people selected for the holiday of a lifetime, there are too many conmen out there to simply take such offers at face value. We are right to be suspicious and, if we are wise, we will always ask for credentials: something that will validate the person and their promise. When it comes to those who make promises in the name of religion, the need for healthy scepticism becomes even greater.

That was certainly the case for the Christians in Colossae. Paul knew enough about what had been happening in that church to realize they had been taken in by people who were promising deeper knowledge and heightened experiences in the life of faith that were undoubtedly attractive, but really were too good to be true. So, before he even begins to address the promises themselves, he addresses the question of who is authorized to make such promises in God's name.

He does so by presenting his own credentials in the very first line of his letter: credentials that carry a threefold endorsement.

The first is the fact he describes himself as 'an apostle of Jesus Christ'. The word 'apostle' in itself had a range of meanings from 'someone who is sent' in a general sense, to someone sent as a missionary in a more specific sense, to one of the men formally designated and sent by Christ to be an apostle in a very narrow sense. It was the latter sense that Paul had in mind as he spoke of himself in this way. Even though he had not been one of the twelve apostles who had been with Jesus from the beginning of his ministry and who had been an eyewitness to the resurrection (*Acts* 1:21-22), nevertheless, he had been added to the apostolic band through his direct encounter with the risen, exalted Lord on the Damascus Road (*1 Cor.* 15:8-10). This unique calling and office

[8]

gave him an authority that came not from himself or his natural abilities, but from Christ.

That in itself would have been sufficient under many circumstances to substantiate his right to speak and for his message to be accepted as being from God, but he adds another strand of authority to his claim. He says his apostolic calling came about 'by the will of God'. It would seem that he says this, not because God's will unfolds even in the tiniest details of life, but rather because his own conversion to Christ and calling into gospel ministry came about through very direct divine intervention. Indeed, by his own confession in what he says to the Corinthians (*1 Cor.* 15:9), despite his academic and personal qualifications, he would have never assumed the office of apostle, or even accepted it from the church, because of his shame over what he had been as a 'persecutor of the church'. It was only because Christ himself had called and commissioned him that he took on the office that had been given to him. As the news of the conversion of this former Pharisee had travelled round the world of the New Testament church, the early Christians would have been well aware that Paul spoke with an authority which had been endorsed by God in a very dramatic manner.

There is a third detail in the way that Paul introduces himself which may well be just a throwaway remark, but which at the same time could carry more than a little weight given the situation to which he was writing. It is the fact that Paul adds in a greeting from 'Timothy our brother'. Timothy had been Paul's travelling companion on a number of occasions and in many ways had become his young protégé in the ministry. In that sense it would not be surprising that he was there with Paul while he was in prison and wished to be remembered to the people in Colossae. But if that was all there was to it, it would have made more sense to simply add that greeting into the final section of the letter where other such greetings would normally be passed on.

It is at least possible that Paul adds Timothy's name in the opening greeting because he is aware of the Jewish background of at least a number of the congregants in this church. It was built into their Jewish psyche to realize that every matter had to be established by two or three witnesses, so for Paul to mention this already respected young minister of the New Testament era as a witness to the fact that Paul was writing, as much as to the content of what he wrote, added an important third credential to its authenticity.

All that may sound very convoluted and remote from our own world; but, given the distance in time and culture between us and this document, there is even more reason for us of all people to know from the outset that this letter has genuine authority. And it is only as we appreciate the care with which that authority was both established and tested in its own day that we can acknowledge its abiding authority through all ages.

CONCERNED, BUT CONFIDENT

It should never fail to amaze us that when Paul writes to Christians who have lost their way in the faith for one reason or another, he is always gentle and patient with them and he always thinks the best of them. Sadly that is far-removed from the harsh and suspicious attitudes that too often prevail among Christians today. So even in the Colossian context, where some extremely serious distortions of the Christian message were being embraced, Paul is extremely gracious in the way he greets this church. He addresses them as 'the saints and faithful brothers in Christ at Colossae' (1:2). That seemingly simple statement is striking on at least three counts.

Even though, as the body of the letter will quickly bring to light, the apostle is genuinely concerned about some of the teachings that were taking hold in this church, his underlying view of it was one of confidence. He regards these Christians as 'saints' or those who were 'holy'. The whole idea of sainthood and saintliness has been hijacked by certain quarters of the professing church through the ages to apply to a supposed elite of super-Christians who are posthumously granted a special status in the church. And, in recognition of their status, they have statues and icons made in their honour and people are encouraged to pray to them. This notion has no foundation whatsoever in biblical teaching and is nothing more than a misguided invention of certain church traditions.

Paul and his fellow-apostles invariably use the expression 'saint' to refer, not to a privileged few within the Christian community, but to all true believers. The word used carried the sense of something or someone who was 'set apart for God'. So, for Paul to address the members of the congregation in Colossae using this term, it is a clear indication that, however much they had lost their way in what they had come to believe and practise, he still firmly believed they were set apart for God. His first word of address sounded a note of confidence in their spiritual standing, as opposed to calling it into question.

This is reinforced by the fact that he goes on to use the adjective 'faithful' as he addresses them as 'brothers'. It would have been enough in itself to have called them brothers – the apostle identifying himself with the people instead of distancing himself from them – but he flags up their faithfulness as he does so. He would, of course, go on to point out the ways in which they were deviating from a faithful understanding of God's truth in the chapters that follow, but that does not disqualify them from still being numbered among the faithful members of God's family.

Once again that speaks volumes to the way we as Christians relate to other professing Christians who, in one way or another, have deviated from the message of Scripture either by ignoring some aspects of its teaching, or by adding to it. The spirit of true Christian discipleship will not be unnecessarily harsh and critical, but, like Priscilla and Aquila as they spoke to Apollos, will seek to explain to them 'the way of God more accurately' (*Acts* 18:26).

The third and most significant expression of Paul's confidence in what God had done and was continuing to do in the life of this church was the fact that he describes them as being 'in Christ'. Even though it might seem more logical to locate them primarily by their geographical setting – 'at Colossae' – he actually does so by means of their spiritual co-ordinates through their union with Christ: the latter being infinitely more important than the former. He will go on almost immediately to show that this expression of optimism about their spiritual state is not empty optimism, but rests on solid grounds. But the fact that he uses this language up front places whatever concerns he had for their beliefs and conduct in the context of a pastoral confidence in their profession of faith.

Church leaders and Christians generally would do well to take a leaf out of the apostle's handbook of pastoral care. Too often we can adopt an adversarial approach in the way we handle fellow-believers who have embraced unusual (or even deviant) teachings and practices, when instead we should do so in the spirit and with an attitude of those who are brothers.

THE BEST THE CHURCH CAN HAVE

The final element in Paul's greeting to the church in Colossae is yet another display of the apostle's genius and creativity as he writes under the direction of the Holy Spirit. The normal salutation a Greek letter-writer would have used at the beginning of their correspondence would have been 'greetings' (*chairein*); but Paul modifies it to 'grace' (*charis*) to convey an altogether different kind of greeting. He deliberately uses a word that speaks of God's favour, not merely prayed for, but conveyed by apostolic authority through the apostolic Word by which God himself was speaking. All the more remarkable because what was happening in the church to which Paul was writing deserved God's disfavour! Yet that is the very essence of God's grace: that through his Son, the Lord Jesus, God favours the disfavoured.

Add to this the fact that Paul also invokes God's 'peace' and the horizons of grace are expanded even further. The particular kind of peace he has in mind is that of *shalom* which was so central to the whole understanding of God's blessing found in the Old Testament. It meant far more than simply being reconciled to God through sins being forgiven and being accepted as righteous through faith in God's promise; but rather to experience the thorough-going, all-round, wellbeing that this fallen world is incapable of providing. Indeed, it is nothing less than a tantalizing foretaste of the wholeness of the world to come in this present age of imperfection.

Again this choice of words on Paul's part is far from insignificant. The whole allure of the false teachers who had inveigled their way into the hearts and minds of the Colossian Christians was the fact they claimed they could offer a brand of Christian experience that was better than what the apostles could provide. Paul's quiet, but overwhelmingly forceful response – completely consistent with Old Testament teaching and promise – was that the experience of salvation offered in the apostolic gospel was nothing less than the very best that God can give. The genuineness of that claim is self-evident, given that it is bound up with the gift of God's own Son to be our Saviour.

The very last detail of this opening word of greeting seals all that has been packed into these two short verses as Paul assures his readers that what is promised comes not merely from 'God' as some remote and faceless deity, but from 'God our Father'. The infinity and eternity of God in all he is as the transcendent One are gloriously enhanced by the intimacy of how he lovingly related to those who trust in him.

It is all too easy for us as twenty-first century readers of the Bible to lose sight of the rich nuances that colour Paul's choice of words even in the seemingly insignificant details of his letters, but which would have spoken strongly to those who were his original readers. Since Paul has begun by making every word count, we can be sure he will go on to make what follows count even more.

2

Credit to Whom Alone It Is Due

We always thank God, the Father of our Lord Jesus Christ, when we pray for you, ⁴ since we heard of your faith in Christ Jesus and of the love that you have for all the saints, ⁵ because of the hope laid up for you in heaven. Of this you have heard before in the word of the truth, the gospel, ⁶ which has come to you, as indeed in the whole world it is bearing fruit and growing – as it also does among you, since the day you heard it and understood the grace of God in truth, ⁷ just as you learned it from Epaphras our beloved fellow servant. He is a faithful minister of Christ on your behalf ⁸ and has made known to us your love in the Spirit. (Col. 1:3-8)

Prayer says a lot about those who claim to be God's people. That is true not just in terms of the content of their prayers, but the way they pray and where and how prayer is woven into the pattern of their lives. Nowhere is that more revealing than in the life and ministry of the apostle Paul. Although prayer is a striking part of the way he ministers to the different churches to whom he writes (we see that from the fact that he never fails to include at least one prayer in his letters to the churches), it is nevertheless fascinating to see where it comes into play.

As he writes to the Colossians, he prays before he begins to address the needs that were arising within the church and, more than that, he offers a prayer of thanksgiving before he offers a prayer for them to be blessed and changed.

There is something quite countercultural in this approach. The normal response to people and situations where there are problems – even where Christians are involved – is to complain before we commend. But the grace of God that Paul has just invoked on behalf of these dear people is precisely the same grace that he conveys in his dealings with them. It is worth teasing out the strands of that grace as he blesses God for the blessings he has not only poured upon the church in Colossae, but which have flowed through it to places and people they had not even heard of.

NOW THANK WE ALL OUR GOD!

Paul begins his letter proper by telling the Colossians how he prays for them. He says that no matter when he prays, he and his fellow workers 'always thank God, the Father of our Lord Jesus Christ' for them. It is striking that this should be the first note he sounds because the reason for his writing this letter is to respond to troubling news of what has been going on in this church. It would have been very easy to have begun in a more ominous tone. In order to understand why he begins in this way, we need to read on.

There is a technique encouraged by those who teach the art of constructive criticism that says a person should be told two positive things about their work before being told something negative. That is not what the apostle is doing here. Rather, his prayer of thanksgiving is a genuine expression of where his confidence about this church lies: in God and in his grace and faithfulness. The fact that he refers to God as 'the God and Father of our Lord Jesus Christ' is a way of pointing not just to what God has done in history through the coming of Christ, but what he has decreed from eternity. In other words, the signs of spiritual life that he has seen in this congregation point back ultimately to what God has purposed in salvation from before the beginning of time.

Many Christians struggle with the idea of a God who is sovereign in salvation, but it is an aspect of God that comes out again and again in the Bible and especially in the writings of Paul. Far from undermining our certainty about salvation, it is intended to do the opposite. And that is precisely the purpose he has in view as he prays for these Christians in Colossae. Although in a real sense the spiritual edifice of the church was shaking because of the false teachings that had crept into its life, the foundation was still secure because it rested in God and his eternal decree which cannot be thwarted. It is for this reason that praise and thanks for the existence of the church in Colossae and for real confidence about its future belonged, not to its leaders or members, but to God alone.

There are very real lessons in that for many churches today. Too often we look to our leaders, our members, our resources and our

[16]

plans and think that they are the key to church life; but that is not the case. It is only as we truly appreciate that were it not for what God planned and purposed in eternity and then fulfilled through the coming of his Son in history, there would be no church and we would have no future. Our thanks are due to him alone.

THE EVIDENCE THAT GOD IS AT WORK

Paul's thanksgiving to God for the church in Colossae is no mere theological nicety, but a response to what he sees in reality in the life of its congregation. He singles out three things in particular that give clear evidence that God was not only responsible for bringing that church into being, but was very much at work in the hearts and lives of its people.

The first is that that he and his co-workers 'have heard of your faith in Christ Jesus' (1:4). Even though Paul had never met these people personally, news about their faith had reached him. It may not seem much to our ears that people were professing faith in Jesus Christ, but in the first century world in which this letter was written, it was a revolutionary stand to take. Despite the religious pluralism and fairly relaxed attitude to the multitude of gods and philosophies that were swirling around at that time, for a person to declare himself or herself as a follower of Christ was to step out on a limb. As Paul said to the Corinthians, the very idea of trusting a 'crucified' Saviour was a stumbling block to Jews and a laughing stock for Gentiles (*1 Cor.* 1:23). So every time Paul heard about people taking a stand for this Jesus, he had reason to rejoice.

The second indicator that God was doing something in the lives of these people is the fact that Paul has not only heard of their faith in Christ, but also of their love 'for all the saints' (1:4). Why should that warrant comment from the apostle? Because a clear sign that God has indeed brought people into his family is that they will not only rejoice in their newfound salvation in a private and personal way in relationship with Christ, but also in that salvation as something they share with all his people. So the fact that the love that characterized the congregation in Colossae was a love that extended to all God's people everywhere said something about its depth and genuineness.

[17]

We should not underestimate the importance of love as a hallmark of the true church. The only distinctive that Jesus ever gave to mark his people off as being truly his was in these words: 'By this all people will know that you are my disciples, if you have love for one another' (*John* 13:35). Little wonder that it warmed Paul's heart to hear of such love in that congregation.

The third sign that caused Paul to believe that God was indeed at work in the church in Colossae was 'the hope laid up for [them] in heaven' on which their faith and love were resting (1:5). When most people hear the word 'hope' they instinctively think in terms of being optimistic that something might happen. However, when Paul uses that term, he does so in the sense of 'quiet certainty'. And the reason he can talk in terms of being sure about what God has promised for the future is because of the fulfillment of all God had promised for the past. Because God's promise of salvation had been fulfilled in a way that defied the wildest dreams of men and angels through God's sending his own dear Son to be our Saviour – more than that, by sending him to the cross in order to secure salvation – then his promise for the future was sealed by all that Christ has done.

For too many people – even some who claim to be Christians – their hope for the future is little more than wishful thinking that can never be strong enough to give them peace as they face their final journey out of this world. But for those whose faith is truly resting on what Christ has done once and for all in the past, they can know a genuine confidence for what is still to come.

THE LIVING AND THE FRUITFUL WORD

It is always fascinating to trace out the train of thought that was going through Paul's mind as he writes in his letters. So as we follow through his line of reasoning in this prayer of thanksgiving, it leads back into 'the word of truth, the gospel' which had come to the Colossians and which they had heard (1:5-6). The power and effectiveness of that message were seen in the faith, love and hope that it had not only borne and continued to bear as fruit in their lives; but which was still 'bearing fruit and growing' all over the world (1:6). Just as a gardener goes out in faith to plant seeds, that look dry and dead in themselves, smiles to himself when he sees them take root, grow and bear fruit; so too this preacher-apostle quietly smiles to himself when he sees the Word of God do its work. This was the apostle who began his most famous exposition of the gospel in Romans by saying, 'I am not ashamed of the gospel, for it is the power of God to salvation for everyone who believes' (*Rom.* 1:16). The church in Colossae was yet another living proof that his confidence in its message was not misplaced.

Even though it was another preacher, Epaphras, who had brought the gospel to Colossae, that in no way diminished Paul's pleasure in seeing this word accomplish God's purpose. Epaphras was not in it for himself any more than Paul was. So, as Epaphras reported the news of what had happened in Colossae to Paul (1:8), it was only that they together might give credit to the One to whom alone it was due, namely God.

It is sad to see ministerial jealousy and rivalry between those who are involved in the work of the gospel. And it is equally sad when churches compete with each other for 'territory' or for people to come and join them. The gospel is continuing to do its work all over the world just as much in our day as it did in Paul's and for that reason we should continue to give thanks to God that, despite our unworthiness and unfaithfulness as his servants, he continues to use his truth to bring people to new life and faith and salvation through his Son.

3

The Prayer that Brings the Letter into Focus

And so, from the day we heard, we have not ceased to pray for you, asking that you may be filled with the knowledge of his will in all spiritual wisdom and understanding, [10] so as to walk in a manner worthy of the Lord, fully pleasing to him, bearing fruit in every good work and increasing in the knowledge of God. [11] May you be strengthened with all power, according to his glorious might, for all endurance and patience with joy, [12] giving thanks to the Father, who has qualified you to share in the inheritance of the saints in light. [13] He has delivered us from the domain of darkness and transferred us to the kingdom of his beloved Son, [14] in whom we have redemption, the forgiveness of sins. (Col. 1:9-14)

One of my enduring memories of a certain teacher I had while at theological seminary was the way he led our classes in prayer before beginning to teach the lesson for the day. In the space of five minutes he would effectively pray through the most important things he wanted us to learn in the hour we were together, but did so in a way that took the teaching to an altogether different level. This was not merely another set of theological truths we needed to get into our heads, but truth for life and which stirred the deepest praise of our hearts. With hindsight, what that teacher was doing in those classes was almost identical to what Paul does in his letters. He prays through the issues he is about to teach, but does so in a way that brings the letters into focus. They identify the most important notes that he will be sounding in all that follows.

As we turn now to Paul's prayer for the Colossians as the prelude to what he is about to write to them, it is more than edifying to see the keynotes he articulates in prayer before exploring what he goes on to expound in the letter itself. He makes it clear that this is not merely a one-off prayer for the occasion, but that he and his fellow workers 'have not ceased to pray' for the Colossians from the first day they heard of their faith (1:9). The essence of his prayers unfolds in three parts followed by a restatement of his grounds for confidence that they will indeed be answered.

WHAT HE PRAYS FOR

The one thing Paul asks for as he remembers this church in Colossae is that the people who are part of it 'may be filled with the knowledge of his [God's] will in all spiritual wisdom and understanding' (1:9). Clearly this concern that dominates his praying has not been plucked at random from the air, or is merely some generic prayer that he offers for Christians everywhere; but, rather, has some bearing on the situation the church in Colossae is facing.

As we read on in his letter we quickly discover that the themes of knowledge, wisdom and understanding crop up at different points along the way and relate to the symptoms of what is going wrong in the church. As we noted in the introduction to the letter, although Paul never formally identifies what the issues were in the church, he gives strong hints that point towards the mysticism and secret knowledge of the local pagan cults that were quietly making inroads into the life and worship of the church. So as Paul tells his original audience the substance of his prayer concerns for them, he hints at those issues in advance in a way that would surely have resonated with them.

The burning question, however, not just for the Colossian Christians, but for Christians through the ages is, 'How do we access God's will and wisdom?' The answer for not a few Christian groupings, as was the case for the church in Colossae, has been through some form of 'deeper knowledge' or 'insight'. But Paul does not allow for that response in the context in which he offers this prayer.

He has already mentioned the way in which the Colossian church came into being in the first place: through what he describes as, 'the word of truth, the gospel' (1:5). It might be tempting for us as those who have the completed Bible in our possession to simply assume that Paul had in mind the gospel as it is expressed in the

New Testament Scriptures; but, of course, that was not entirely the case. We forget too easily that, for the greater part of its history, the New Testament church did not actually have the New Testament in its hand. The bulk of preaching and teaching they would have heard was from the Old Testament as it was expounded in light of Christ's coming as the fulfillment of all it promised. And then gradually over the years, the different books and letters of what we now call the New Testament would have been added to that corpus of writings recognized and received by the church as having come from God.

Paul's point is this: the same word of truth through which these people had been brought to faith, was the same word of truth by which they would grow towards maturity and usefulness in the life of faith. And that has been the enduring principle of conversion and spiritual growth through the ages. Peter makes precisely that point in what he says about the role of God's word in new birth and spiritual growth (*1 Pet.* 1:22-2:3).

It is often tempting to think that the Bible is not enough to bring us into the fullness of what we are meant to be as Christians; but again and again it reminds us that under normal circumstances, the Holy Spirit uses his living word to do just that. It is not something extra that we need, but a fuller appreciation of what we have already been given.

WHERE IT LEADS

It is important to realize that Paul does not pray for this knowledge of God's will through his Word as an end in itself. If hearing God's word read and proclaimed becomes an exercise in self-gratification, it has not accomplished what God intends through it. Paul makes it clear that his prayer for an increase in knowledge and wisdom has a purpose in view: so that his readers would 'walk in a manner worthy of the Lord, fully pleasing to him, bearing fruit in every good work and increasing in the knowledge of God' (1:10).

The essence of this clause in Paul's prayer distills into the statement that the Colossians might 'walk in a manner worthy of the Lord'. By that he means that they would live in a way that is consistent with their newfound relationship with God and with life in his family. Just as bearing the family name in a very human sense is

[23]

bound up with upholding the family honour, so in an even greater sense is bearing God's name as those who are part of the church. Being a Christian in the biblical sense of the term always has an ethical dimension to it. We cannot be Christians in name only, it must reshape the kind of people we are and reorder the way we live.

What is stated in shorthand in that clause is spelled out more fully first of all in terms of living in a way that is 'fully pleasing to him [God]'. That is a telling remark. All too often people embrace the Christian faith for self-gratifying reasons, only to find that it doesn't work. The reason for this is that self-gratifying Christianity is never satisfying. It is only when we realize that salvation delivers us from that deeply-ingrained instinct in our sinful nature to live to please ourselves and liberate us for a life that pleases God that we discover where true satisfaction in life is actually found.

It follows, therefore, that a life lived for God's pleasure will be a life that becomes fruitful in God's service and which will continue to grow to know God in a richer, deeper way. Here again the very language that Paul uses is tailored to address the issues that were surfacing in Colossae indirectly and gently, before going on to wrestle with them more overtly in the main body of the letter. The Colossians' desire for a deeper experience of God would not be found through ritual and self-denial, but through discovering more of who he is and what he is like as he has revealed himself in his word. In that sense, knowledge and experience of God are inseparably joined, because it is as we respond to him by faith and obedience that we enter more fully into the enjoyment of God himself and that in turn leads us into an enjoyment of life as he meant it to be lived.

HOW IT WORKS

Once again, as we follow through the contours of Paul's prayer, we cannot help but notice how he prayerfully covers in advance the issues he will go on to address more directly in what he says. As people in general and Christians in particular grapple with the question, 'How can we be changed?' both groups are prone to the wrong kind of answers (nearly all of which come down to some sort of self-reformation). In light of that, Paul's answer is extremely significant.

He talks in the first place about the need for strength and power to change and makes it clear that mere human resources are not enough to bring about change that is real. So he rightly points to God's 'glorious might' as being the power outside ourselves that is needed if we are to go the distance in the Christian life (1:9). But that statement, if left to stand alone, could easily be misunderstood in terms of what really makes a person a Christian.

It is crucial, therefore, that we see how it links in to the following statement: 'giving thanks to the Father who has qualified us to share in the inheritance of the saints of light' (1:12). He is, of course, making the point which he makes more fully elsewhere, that although we by nature and because of our sin are disqualified from having a place in God's family and from a relationship with him, God in his grace has qualified us for both, not through any merit we have ourselves, but through the salvation he provides in Christ.

To use the technical terms that Paul uses elsewhere, he is talking here about our being justified and our being sanctified through our union with Christ. In other words, he is reminding us that it is not merely the power to live a life that pleases God that is needed for a place among his people, but that the demands of his justice should be satisfied as well. So the joy and thankfulness that Paul prays for in this context spring directly from what God has so freely and graciously provided through his Son for all who will believe in him.

In that sense, this section of Paul's prayer addresses and answers the two great questions that confront anyone who genuinely wants to find new life in fellowship with God: 'How do I get in?' and 'How do I keep it up?' On both counts we are pointed to Christ.

WHY HE CAN BE SURE

Given all that Paul knew about the situation in Colossae, it is not hard to see that the requests he makes for these people as he prays are pretty weighty. What gives Paul the confidence that his prayer will be heard, let alone answered? The answer comes in its closing sentence: 'He has delivered us from the domain of darkness and transferred us to the kingdom of his beloved Son, in whom we have redemption, the forgiveness of sins' (1:13-14). Including himself in the prayer for the first time and aligning himself with

[25]

these believers who he has already acknowledged as having a faith that is genuine, he uses the past tense to point to what God has done once and for all through his Son.

It is very tempting to read these words merely in terms of the personal experience of someone who has become a Christian, and there is a sense in which that is both understandable and true. When anyone comes to faith there is indeed a radical renewal that takes place in them. But to see Christian conversion merely in such private and personal terms is to lose sight of a far more important dimension that underpins salvation as a whole. That is, salvation is not merely about what God does in us through his Son and by his Spirit, but what he did for us through the cross.

In that sense the bedrock of Christian assurance lies, not in when and how a person professed their faith in Jesus Christ, but in all that Jesus Christ did for his people once and for all, supremely on the cross. It was there and then on Calvary that God delivered all his people from the dominion of darkness and transferred them into the kingdom of his Son. And it was there and then that he secured their redemption and the forgiveness of their sins.

It may sound like hair-splitting to make that distinction between what happened at a specific point in space and time on the cross and what happens at a particular point in one's personal experience, but it has enormous relevance to the whole focus of our life and how that affects our experience of life. The Colossians were being steered towards what we might call an existential form of Christianity that was fixated with subjective individual experience, but the gospel (without minimizing the place of subjective experience) points to the cross as the objective focus of faith through which true experience is found.

Given the weight of what Paul prays in this prayer and the intricate flow of concern that unfolds through it, we begin to get a feel for where he is going as he prepares to address the issues the Colossians (and indeed all Christians) need to hear.

4

Lord of the Cosmos, Head of the Church

He is the image of the invisible God, the firstborn of all creation.
[16] For by him all things were created, in heaven and on earth, visible
and invisible, whether thrones or dominions or rulers or authorities –
all things were created through him and for him. [17] And he is before
all things, and in him all things hold together. [18] And he is the head
of the body, the church. He is the beginning, the firstborn from the
dead, that in everything he might be preeminent. [19] For in him all the
fullness of God was pleased to dwell, [20] and through him to reconcile
to himself all things, whether on earth or in heaven, making peace by
the blood of his cross. (Col. 1:15-20)

Paul's prayer for the Colossians in the preceding section touches
on the concerns that were troubling them with deep pastoral
sensitivity. The things he prays that God will give them are the
very things that they felt were missing from their newfound life
and experience in the Christian faith – a sense of deficiency that
in all likelihood had been fostered by the false teachers in their
midst. As we have suggested several times already, these teachers
were subtly suggesting that the Christ in whom they had believed
through the gospel was not enough to meet these deficiencies and
so were offering other things to fill the gap.

Paul's prayer has already begun to challenge these notions, in
part through his asking that God would indeed 'fill' them with all
that was needed in the life of faith; but, more significantly, pointing to Christ as the one in whom that fullness is found. Through
him they are 'qualified... to share in the inheritance of the saints
in light' (1:12), are 'delivered... from the domain of darkness and
transferred... to the kingdom of his Son' (1:13), because it is in
Christ that 'we have redemption, the forgiveness of sins' (1:14).
It is impossible to overstate the scale of blessing that is bound up
in those three statements – something that went far beyond the

expectations that were being stirred among the Colossians by those who were quietly undermining the gospel they had heard from Epaphras. The depth and quality of life they were suppos- edly missing out on was more than available in the life promised in Christ. In essence, the one thing that alienates us from the true life for which we were created as human beings is the fact that we have been estranged from our Creator through our sin in all its dimensions. So, Paul is arguing, if we can be redeemed – set free at a price – from our sin and its consequence and be brought back into fellowship with God, then the life for which we were destined becomes ours.

In praying such a prayer and making such great claims, Paul is throwing down the gauntlet to those who were preaching a different message in Colossae. The question then becomes, 'On what basis can such claims be made?' And that implied question becomes the link that takes us seamlessly into what follows in this section as Paul moves from talking about 'the Son in whom we have redemption' (1:14) to opening our eyes to who he actually is. In so doing he leads us into one of the most extraordinary paragraphs in the Bible.

It is extraordinary because it has the capacity to overwhelm the mind of the finest Bible scholar and yet at the same time stir the heart of the humblest believer as Paul draws aside the curtain momentarily to allow us a glimpse of the glory of Christ.

When we lived in London we used to visit the National Gallery in Trafalgar Square from time to time. Every time we went we were always struck by the fact that while on the one hand there were art experts engrossed in the mechanics and detail of the great paint- ings on display, there were also hordes of schoolchildren who were transfixed by the same paintings, even though their knowledge of them was scant. Whatever they may not have known, they certainly knew they were in the presence of greatness. So here, Paul knows full well that even he cannot fully fathom the mysteries of which he writes in relation to Christ; but he knows this: he and his readers are in the presence of majestic greatness of an altogether different order as they reflect on who he is.

It is more than a little significant to see the way that Paul chooses to approach the problem at Colossae. He does not begin by pointing the finger at those who were subverting the gospel in that church, or even exposing the specific false teachings they were spreading. Instead, he brings his readers face to face with Christ in all his glory in a way that simply speaks for itself. When Christ is set forth in all his majestic splendour, the sheer weight of truth and glory that are his has its own unique ability to deal with all that would try to question him.

Many aspects of this section would suggest that it is a hymn, or at least poetic in its form. If that is the case, then it is an entirely appropriate way to try to express the inexpressible and take us beyond the limits of what reason can grasp to where only faith can lead. That is not for a moment to suggest that what Paul says here about Christ is unreasonable; simply that it is beyond the scope of mere reason, but nevertheless makes absolute sense in light of the world and universe in which we live. Without being over-simplistic as we try to open up what Paul says, there are three main components to his description of Christ – each of which undergirds the claims and promises he has linked to Christ in the prayer he has just offered for these Christians.

LORD OF CREATION

Paul's references to Christ so far have been in relation to him as the Lord of Salvation, but, as we have seen, questions were being raised in Colossae as to whether or not the salvation he offered was enough. As Paul now brings us face to face with Christ in all his fullness, he shows that his greatness as Lord of salvation is rooted in the fact that he is actually Lord of all creation. I have never ceased to be surprised by the fact that some of the most powerful and influential people in the world often appear unimpressive in themselves and it is only when we are allowed to get to know them that we discover there is literally 'more to them than meets the eye'. And that is what is happening here. Paul allows the 'unimpressive' Jesus who was being quietly questioned in this church to step out of the shadows and be seen for who he really is; and his credentials are unsurpassable.

He is the 'image of the invisible God' (1:15). Paul is clearly reaching for the language we find at the very beginning of the Bible to describe the creation of Adam and Eve. They were made in the 'image' and 'likeness' of God (*Gen.* 1:26). There have been many ideas put forward to try and capture what that means in real terms, but in its simplest form it meant that man was meant to reflect in the created world what God is in all his uncreated greatness. Man was intended to be God-like as he made God known to the world. So when Paul uses this language in relation to Christ, at the very least he is thinking about the way Jesus makes God known. There may well be other layers of significance packed into this description as well, but there is not space to explore them here.

The fact that Paul chooses to refer to God as the 'invisible God' may also be significant, in that the teachers who were influencing the Colossian church seem to have been leaning towards mystical ways of getting to know God, so Paul deliberately chooses words that challenge their ideas about how we can 'see' the invisible.

Paul also describes Christ as 'the firstborn of all creation' in this verse. A group in the early church under the influence of Arius in the 4th Century latched on to this language to claim that Jesus was not the eternal Son of God, but was a created being – something the Jehovah's Witnesses still claim today. However, even from the wider context of this verse, that is clearly not what Paul is suggesting. Rather, he is using the culturally appropriate language of rank and privilege of the day to speak of Christ's pre-eminence over the entire created order.

He goes on in the next verse to elaborate on this great statement about Christ by saying, 'For by him all things were created...' (1:16). He was God's agent in the act of creation – something that is echoed by John in the opening verses of his Gospel (*John* 1:3). Clearly Paul is speaking about what Christ was before he took human flesh and entered our world, but the way he is crafting this word-portrait makes it clear that it is the same incarnate Christ he has in view.

Even in this angle that Paul gives on the identity of Christ, he still has the Colossian detractors of Christ in view. The particular details he chooses to highlight – the extent of the created order which owes its origin to Christ, and the fact that he punctuates this verse with the repetition of 'all things' – are a pointed response to the very things that were being presented as authorities in their own right by the false teachers.

If these two monumental statements about Christ were not enough in themselves to establish his claim to lordship over the cosmos, Paul adds a third: 'And he is before all things, and in him all things hold together' (1:17). His being 'before all things' is another way of highlighting Christ's supremacy, but the second part of the verse is an even more astonishing reiteration of that fact. Paul is in effect saying that Christ is the unsustained sustainer of everything. In other words, Christ's supremacy is seen not merely in his involvement in God's work of creation, but also in his work of providence in which he upholds and governs the entire universe.

The implied question that Paul is answering in all of this – over against the ideas that were spreading in Colossae – was 'Who has the authority to claim they can make God known?' The false teachers in the church were looking to powers within the created order; but Paul takes us to the One who is above it.

HEAD OF THE CHURCH

Having succinctly asserted and established Christ's authority over all things generally, in the next verse Paul goes on to assert his lordship over the church specifically. 'And he is the head of the body, the church' (1:18).

The Bible uses the expression 'head of' in different ways in different places. Often it is used in the sense of being 'head of a corporation' to mean 'in charge of' something. Although it is certainly true that Christ is 'in charge of' the church as its sole King and Head – and Paul states that elsewhere – that isn't what he has in view here. Rather, he is thinking of what a person's head is to their body by way of dependence. Decapitate a person and their body is lifeless. Separate the church as a body from Christ as its head and it becomes a lifeless institution and not the living organism it is meant to be. Too often the church looks to 'other things' to inject life and vitality into it; when what it really needs is to appreciate its need for meaningful communion with Christ.

However, once again Paul elaborates on what he is saying. The headship of Christ also means that he is 'the beginning, the first-born from the dead'. Paul's choice of words echo those already used to describe Christ's relation to the original creation in the preceding verses and is meant to make us think more deeply about the church as God's new creation. The word 'beginning' carries the sense of 'source of' and the expression 'firstborn from the dead' points to the significance of Christ's resurrection. Put together they combine to speak of the whole new order that God has created through his saving grace in Christ in the lives of his people – something that is bound up ultimately with what Jesus calls 'the renewal of all things' (*Matt.* 19:28).

Christ is not only Lord over the cosmos in its entirety, despite its present fallen state; he is also Lord over the renewed cosmos that has already begun through the new life he has given to his people, the church. And, since that is the case, the church should not allow herself to be distracted (as was the case in Colossae) by looking elsewhere for life and vitality when it is found in Christ alone.

GOD IN HUMAN FLESH

The last two verses of this section draw together the great assertions that Paul has been making about Christ in what he has been saying so far as he explains who Christ is and what he has done.

'For in him all the fullness of God was pleased to dwell' (1:19). This is not an easy verse to translate and it arguably makes better sense if we follow the *New International Version's*, 'God was pleased to have all his fullness dwell in him'. Either way, Paul is clearly speaking about God's purpose in the incarnation of his Son. He is picking up on that great truth of the gospel expressed by John when he said, 'And the Word became flesh and dwelt among us, and we have seen his glory, the glory as of the only Son from the Father, full of grace and truth' (*John* 1:14), a truth that Paul restates in the next chapter (2:9).

Once again the apostle is deliberate in his choice and use of words. The longing for fullness among these Colossian Christians, that he knew was being agitated by the newcomers in their midst, would surely resonate with the ultimate fullness of God himself revealed in the incarnate Christ. There is no greater fullness than that which belongs to God and is made known and freely offered in Christ, so it would be the height of foolishness to think we can look to someone or something else to find genuine fulfillment for ourselves.

Paul puts the finest of all possible points on this as he draws the threads of this section together with the words: '...and through him to reconcile to himself all things, whether on earth or in heaven, making peace by the blood of his cross' (1:20). It is not merely that Christ is God and has the power to meet our deepest needs and longings in life; but that he is God our Saviour and has done all that was required to allow God to pour his fullest blessing into our lives! The sheer baldness of Paul's description of the heart of Christ's work of salvation – 'by the blood of his cross' – is a stark reminder of the depth and seriousness of our sin and its consequences. The fact that he brings his Christian readers back to the cross as the key to their full enjoyment of the Christian life is staggeringly significant. Too often through the history of the church there has been a mentality among Christians that effectively says, 'The cross gets me into God's family, but I need something else to take me into it more deeply'.

Nothing could be further from the truth. Paul in the most potent way imaginable in these verses brings home to us the lengths to which God had go in order to secure redemption for his people and for the world and universe that he has made. And that leads us into what Paul goes on to say next.

5

No Greater Salvation

And you, who once were alienated and hostile in mind, doing evil deeds, ²² he has now reconciled in his body of flesh by his death, in order to present you holy and blameless and above reproach before him, ²³ if indeed you continue in the faith, stable and steadfast, not shifting from the hope of the gospel that you heard, which has been proclaimed in all creation under heaven, and of which I, Paul, became a minister.
(Col. 1:21-23)

One of the recurring mistakes that preachers make is to take their listeners to dizzy heights of God's truth revealed in Scripture, only to leave them wondering how they relate to everyday people in their everyday lives. The apostle Paul could never be accused of that!

He has indeed just taken his readers into the very stratosphere of biblical truth as he has drawn aside the veil to reveal the greatness and majesty of Jesus; but he will not allow his audience to be mere spectators. He wants not just the congregation in Colossae, but Christians everywhere to realize that the great truth about Jesus in terms of who he is and what he has done must have a great impact on those who genuinely put their trust in him. The greatness of the Saviour presented to us in the gospel must, by definition, have an impact on the greatness of the salvation promised in that same gospel.

Paul has already declared his conviction that those who professed faith in Colossae were indeed genuine Christians and he has given thanks for the evidence of their new life in Christ. So here as he teases out what he has been saying about Christ, Paul relates it directly to the life and experience of these believers.

He does so in a way that is typical for the apostles by looking at salvation from three different angles in order to see that it is invariably greater than we could ever imagine. To borrow the language used in Hebrews, it is 'such a great salvation' (*Heb.* 2:3) that there really is nothing that can compare to it.

At one level Paul is obviously speaking to people who are Christians, but who are struggling with doubts and questions about their faith – in particular, Christians like those in Colossae who are suffering from what might be called, 'Something's Missing Syndrome'. They have put their faith in Christ, but quickly realize that their new life of faith is often far from straightforward and they are easy prey to those who say that they need something more to find fulfillment. What such Christians need is not something extra, but to appreciate how much they have already been given in Christ. There have been and will always be many such people in the church.

At another level, however, there is a much wider group of people to whom Paul is speaking, albeit indirectly. That is, the rest of humanity who spend their lives looking for salvation/redemption/ deliverance/life in every imaginable sphere but are frustrated in their quest. However 'great' the life promised through prosperity, power, pleasure or popularity, philosophy, piety, or whatever; it is never great enough to carry us from the cradle to the grave and into eternity. To them Paul says there is one life that can and it is the life and salvation that are found in Christ. He can make this claim for three important reasons.

IT DEALS WITH OUR PAST

As we have indicated already, Paul does not allow his Colossian listeners to be mere spectators to what he has just been saying about Christ and all that he has done. Unlike those visitors to the National Gallery we spoke of in the last chapter who were merely spectators to something great, these Colossian Christians were participants in Christ and his great salvation. So the apostle links what he has been saying about Christ and how he secured salvation to his readers and what that salvation meant for them.

He begins, as he so often does in such situations, by reminding these people of what they used to be. They once were 'alienated and hostile in mind, doing evil deeds' (1:21). Brief and all as that statement may sound to our ears; it is a penetrating analysis of what has sometimes been called 'the human condition'. It explains the state we are in by nature in our life without God.

We are 'alienated'. Interestingly Paul does not qualify that statement, but simply says that a sense of alienation is something that has haunted human beings since time immemorial. We feel estranged, dislocated, at odds with people, at odds with our environment and even with ourselves. It is something that philosophers have pondered, writers have explored and poets and composers have mused on; but Paul says only the Bible can explain it. The root of our many-faceted alienation lies in our alienation from God. Before he sinned, Adam knew no such estrangement from God, his wife, his world or himself; but after he sinned he knew all four. He had been forewarned by God that this was what would happen if he chose to sin – if he ate the fruit of the tree of the knowledge of good and evil he would 'surely die' (*Gen.* 2:17). He would 'die' in the sense that he would begin to experience the disintegration of life as God meant it to be: his relationship with God his creator would be ruptured, as would his relationships with Eve his wife, the world as his home and even with himself in his own sense of who he really was. He would experience alienation in time that would lead to alienation for eternity if it could not be reversed.

In a very real sense the story of the human race from that point onwards has been one of endless attempts to reverse that deep-seated estrangement. From Adam's reaching for a 'fig-leaf' to cover his shame before God right through to the multitude of religions that claim we can somehow claw our way back into God's favour, they all prove futile.

That had been the story of these people in Colossae until the day Epaphras came back to them with the message that they could be reconciled to God – their estrangement be reversed – not through what they might try to do for God, but through all that he had done for them in his Son, the Lord Jesus.

The second component of what had been wrong with these people in their natural condition as human beings was that they were 'hostile in mind' – Paul's implication being that their hostility was directed towards God. The sin of Adam went far beyond a mistake that he could not undo, to damage to himself that he was unable to repair. From that point on in his life it was no longer his nature to

[37]

delight in God and in pleasing him; instead he delighted in himself and in his self-gratification. All of which meant that his mind was now set against God instead of being in submission to him.

So endemic is this hostility of the human mind towards God that even his best efforts to reach God through religion have failed for one simple reason: it has been religion on man's terms and not God's. That too had been where these Colossian Christians once had been.

The third element in the seriousness of the human problem that Paul identifies – and it is an inevitable consequence of the two he has mentioned already – is that it leads to a life of 'doing evil deeds'. A life that is estranged from God and a mind that is hostile to God can only mean that people will by nature do what is right and pleasing in their own eyes instead of what is right and pleasing in the sight of God.

The terseness and brevity of Paul's diagnosis of what is wrong with our race belie the depth and seriousness of what that diagnosis implies. It not only makes it clear that such a state of revolt against God must have grave consequences, but more than that, it is beyond our power and ability as human beings to put things right.

Yet, as Paul addresses these Colossians in light of who Christ is and what he has done on the cross and in particular in light of the fact they had put their faith in this Christ, he can assure them that their past was dealt with. It was not merely that they were no longer liable for what they had done, but that they no longer were what they used to be. Such is the greatness of the salvation promised in the gospel that all who look to Christ in faith are truly and utterly set free from their past life.

IT TRANSFORMS OUR PRESENT

Given what Paul has said already about the impact of Christ's redeeming work on the past for these people, it should go without saying that his work has equally great implications for their present as well. If their standing before God in their previous state was one of alienation and condemnation, then their new standing in Christ had to be radically different if they were to have genuine hope and peace of mind. And that is exactly what the apostle assures them of as he tells them, 'he has now reconciled [you] in his body of flesh by his death, in order to present you holy and blameless and above reproach before him' (1:22).

The primary focus of this statement is the legal standing a person has as a Christian before God. It is clear that though they had once been judicially estranged from God by virtue of their sin and guilt – their sin had made them liable to God's judgment – through Christ they were now 'reconciled'. What is also clear is that this had come about, not through anything Christ had done in them (making them better people), but what Christ had done for them 'in his body of flesh by his death' on the cross. The upshot of this is that he [Christ] may then 'present you holy and blameless and above reproach before him [God]'. The scenario is that of Judgment Day and the word Paul uses for 'present' is one that was used to present someone before a court. And the implication is that a person can know in the present what the verdict will be in the future when they stand before the court of heaven. If their faith is in Christ then they can rest assured that they will be justified before that court: not on the basis of their own merit and record, but on Christ's presented on their behalf.

There are, of course, other vital dimensions to the greatness of the salvation promised in Christ to all who believe; but having highlighted the sharp edge of human sin and fallenness, Paul deliberately highlights the antidote that God has provided through his own Son and the sacrifice he offered on the cross. As Paul so rightly says elsewhere, for all who are trusting in Christ for their salvation, 'There is therefore now no condemnation for those who are in Christ Jesus' (*Rom.* 8:1). Their past of living under condemnation has been exchanged for a present in which they are fully accepted by God as righteous and forgiven on account of all that Christ provides through his righteous life and his atoning death.

IT IS SUFFICIENT FOR OUR FUTURE

There is, however, a qualification in what Paul says to the Colossians. What he has outlined in the preceding verses will be true for them, '...if indeed you continue in the faith, stable and steadfast, not shifting from the hope of the gospel that you heard, which has been proclaimed in all creation under heaven, and of which I, Paul, became a minister' (1:23). The 'if' in that sentence looms large on the horizon of everything the apostle has said so far in this letter, but not in the way some people have imagined.

Some Bible teachers take this little word to imply that it is possible for a Christian to lose his or her salvation. That, in the case of the Colossians, having affirmed the genuineness of their conversion experience at the beginning of the letter, Paul is now telling them that they could lose their salvation as quickly as they found it; but to read it in that way would run counter not only to what Paul teaches so clearly elsewhere, but what he affirms so definitively in his prayer (1:12-14).

The 'if' that Paul inserts at this point is there to remind his readers that there is a very real difference between Christian faith that is real and a faith that is false. The Bible warns repeatedly and Christ himself warns most pointedly that there are many who claim to be his followers with their lips, but whose claim is contradicted by their lives. Paul is not suggesting that the Colossians have made a false claim to faith (he has already thanked God in prayer for the widely recognized evidence that their faith is genuine); but rather he is reminding them that genuineness of that faith will prove itself by not being sidetracked by the new teachings they are hearing.

What he is seeking to impress on his hearers crystallizes in his saying, '...not shifting from the hope of the gospel that you heard, which has been proclaimed in all creation under heaven, and of which I, Paul, became a minister'. The 'gospel' they were hearing from the teachers who had come in among them was a different gospel from the one that had come to them from Paul via Epaphras – the gospel which had already been universally proclaimed – and was in reality no gospel at all.

The greatness of the salvation that is promised in the gospel cannot be separated from the greatness of the Saviour that gospel proclaims. Any attempt in the first century world of Paul's day or the twenty-first century of our world to add to or subtract from the Christ who is that Saviour is a message that cannot save.

6

Recognizing Faithful Ministry

Now I rejoice in my sufferings for your sake, and in my flesh I am filling up what is lacking in Christ's afflictions for the sake of his body, that is, the church, ^{25} of which I became a minister according to the stewardship from God that was given to me for you, to make the word of God fully known, ^{26} the mystery hidden for ages and generations but now revealed to his saints. ^{27} To them God chose to make known how great among the Gentiles are the riches of the glory of this mystery, which is Christ in you, the hope of glory. ^{28} Him we proclaim, warning everyone and teaching everyone with all wisdom, that we may present everyone mature in Christ. ^{29} For this I toil, struggling with all his energy that he powerfully works within me. (Col. 1:24-29)

It is always both fascinating and intriguing to see the way that Paul's train of thought unfolds and his argument develops in his letters, because both are always geared to winning the hearts of his hearers as well as persuading their minds. Too often the great apostle is seen only as the great preacher-theologian of the New Testament world – which he clearly is – but he is also the great pastor-theologian. He knows that he is not merely dealing with the message God has entrusted to him, but also with the people to whom that message must come. And that in many ways explains how Paul makes the transition into this next section of this letter.

He knows that there is a spiritual battle for hearts and minds being waged in Colossae and that the competing messages that are circulating in the church there cannot be separated from the messengers through whom they come. It is not just that the new message that these people were hearing claimed to offer more than the message they had first believed, but that its messengers were clearly excellent communicators (2:4). So the issue at stake as the church is faced with the decision of which they should follow boils down to which bears the marks of authenticity. And that is the point at which Paul steps into their dilemma in a rather unusual way. He does something that is quite out of character for the apostle: he talks about himself and his ministry – not in any way to attract attention to himself, but rather to his message.

What he wants his readers to reflect on is this: 'What kind of message is worth the kind of suffering that he and his fellow apostles have faced in order to make it known?' Unlike those who were gaining ground among the Colossian Christians, his ministry had come at significant personal cost. So, what does that say, not merely about him, but also the message for which he was so willing to suffer?

A JOY TO SUFFER FOR

Paul was not merely willing to suffer for the message he was proclaiming, but he rejoiced in his sufferings (1:24). Straightaway his readers are stopped in their tracks and made to wonder what is going on with this man. Either he has taken leave of his senses and become entangled in one of those bizarre cults that take pleasure in self-inflicted pain, or else he is a man of extraordinary conviction.

One does not have to dig very deep into Paul's life and labour to realize that the first option carries no weight. The apostle never sought suffering and the sufferings he experienced were not some form of cultic ritual. They were inflicted upon him by those who were opposed to his message.

That leaves us then with the second option. Here was a man who was so gripped by the message he was proclaiming that he was not just willing, but eager to suffer for it and within a few short years he would be willing to die for it. He had an overwhelming conviction that his message was not merely true; it was the Truth. And what was true for Paul was consistent with all the other New Testament apostles who also suffered and almost all of whom were martyred for their faith.

That fact is not just a sobering detail of early Christian history; it is actually something that brings us to the very heart of what is worthwhile in this transient world and life of ours. Someone has rightly said, 'If something is worth living for, it is worth dying for' and that has been proved true in many worthy wars and causes in the history of the world. But it is the prominence this has in the story of the Christian Church that takes it to a different level, for two reasons. One is that the call to suffering for the sake of the gospel is for all Christians and not just Christian ministers and missionaries (*Mark* 8:34; *2 Tim.* 3:12). The other is that it is suffering not only for a good cause in this world; but for something worth having in the next.

What is especially intriguing about Paul's comments on his sufferings, however, is that he says, 'and in my flesh I am filling up what is lacking in Christ's afflictions for the sake of his body, that is, the church' (1:24). This statement has raised more than a few eyebrows. How can there be anything that is lacking in the sufferings of Christ?

The answer, of course, is that there is nothing deficient in the sufferings Christ endured in order to secure redemption for his people. That is clear from the fact that his dying words on the cross declared his work 'accomplished' (*John* 19:30) and also from the way Paul presents the suffering and death of Christ as being sufficient for salvation. Paul is not suggesting that he somehow adds to the finished work of Christ in redemption through his own afflictions.

Instead it would seem that Paul is thinking of the afflictions of Christ in relation to 'his body, that is, the church'. Jesus warned his disciples in advance that being one of his followers would necessarily involve trouble and hardship (*John* 16:33) and that was borne out through the entire New Testament, both through its teaching and in its record of the sufferings that became the hallmark of the church. And it was in that sense that Paul was so willing to joyfully endure the suffering that was part and parcel of the life of faith. The message of gospel was so great it was a joy to suffer for it.

A PRIVILEGE TO SERVE

It stands to reason that if Paul counted it a joy to suffer for the sake of this message, he also saw it as a wonderful privilege to be its servant. In the next verse he describes himself as a 'minister' of the church, not in the sense of being ordained to office, but as one who serves the church. But what he means by that is qualified by the way he has used that same terminology in a previous verse where he describes himself as a servant of the gospel (1:23). His servant ministry in the church is inseparably bound up with his being a servant minister of the Word.

When we appreciate that connection, then we realize that Paul's willingness to suffer and be snubbed in the work he was doing among the church in its widest sense was fueled by the high sense of privilege in his being called to proclaim God's message. He did not assume this responsibility on his own initiative, but was made a steward of it by God himself in the commission he received on the day of his conversion on the Damascus Road (*Acts* 26:15-18). This once proud Pharisee who was so opposed to the gospel and the church became the humble, self-sacrificing servant of both because he saw it as his greatest privilege to serve their common Lord.

A MYSTERY FROM ANOTHER WORLD

Paul's view of this message he was called to serve was so high that he was committed to make it 'fully known' (1:25). The NIV rendering, 'to present to you the word of God in all its fullness', perhaps captures the sense a little better. The Colossians were seeking 'fullness' and Paul has already been dropping more than subtle hints to the end that true fullness is already in their possession, even though it is not yet fully their experience and its key is found in God's Word.

Paul opens up the horizons of that fullness of God's message when he describes it as 'the mystery hidden for ages and generations but now revealed to his saints' (1:26). His use of the word 'mystery' has a double edge to it. On the one hand it was a cultic word that was gaining prominence in the New Testament world in relation to so-called mystery religions that involved initiation rites and inner circles – the kind of influences that were common in the region around Colossae and were being dressed in some cases in 'Christian' clothing. On the other hand, he was using the term with a very biblical sense: namely as an expression for important truth that was beyond the reach of finite, fallen human reason, but which God himself was pleased to reveal to 'his saints' – that is, to those he has 'set apart' for himself through salvation.

In that sense, the message of the gospel really is a mystery from another world, because it comes from God. But it is only when we hear how Paul expresses the mystery that we appreciate how utterly other-worldly it really is. He says, 'To them God chose to make known how great among the Gentiles are the riches of the glory of this mystery, which is Christ in you, the hope of glory' (1:27). There is some debate as to whether the 'great' in what Paul is saying applies to the 'riches of this glory' or to the fact that they are being proclaimed among the Gentiles. I am inclined, over against the ESV's translation to think the former.

The greatness of the glory of this mystery of the gospel – which was first entrusted to the Jewish people – is indeed in part the fact that it includes the Gentiles as well. Abraham was told by God that in him 'all the families of the earth would be blessed' (*Gen.* 12:3). But it was the essence of that blessing, rather than its global scope that constituted its greatness and Paul identifies that here: it is 'Christ in you, the hope of glory' (1:27). That is, the mystery of gospel as it is proclaimed in this world is the certainty of glory in the next for all who believe it. And that certainty is found in being united to Christ.

It is easy to struggle with the concept of 'glory' in a passage like this. We know that word Paul uses speaks of brightness and weight, but it is still hard to conceptualize what it actually looks like. One clue is found in Romans where Paul talks about the damage done by sin in the well-known verse, 'for all have sinned and fall short of the glory of God' (3:23), in which 'glory of God' almost certainly refers to the image of God in Adam before he sinned. Paul's statement there is a kind of photographic negative (for those who remember the old way of taking photographs) to what he expresses here to the Colossians. The inglorious humanity that became Adam's and ours after the fall is exchanged for a glorious new humanity through union with Christ in salvation, which in turn will be exchanged for a glorified humanity when Jesus returns.

When we begin to see the mystery of the gospel from that angle, then we start to see its other-worldly dimensions in an altogether different way.

A MESSAGE THAT TRANSFORMS

That perspective leads naturally into the last two comments Paul offers by way of explanation and vindication of his ministry and message. Since it is Christ who is the key to the hope of glory, so it is Christ alone whom Paul proclaims. He refuses to add to that message or subtract anything from it, because Christ is all-sufficient.

It is interesting to notice the dynamics involved in preaching Christ include, rebuking, teaching and presenting people 'mature in Christ' (1:28). Those same dynamics are highlighted by Paul in what he says to Timothy as being of the essence of how God's Word works in people's lives (*2 Tim.* 3:16-17) and also as the contours of a truly Word-based ministry (*2 Tim.* 4:2). It will always involve rebuke and instruction and it will always be geared to restoring broken lives to what God meant them to be.

It is interesting also to see Paul's deliberate repetition of 'everyone' in this verse. In a church that was being infected with spiritual elitist tendencies of those who had been initiated into certain 'mysteries' over against those who had not, the apostle is reminding his readers that the Christ of the gospel is for everyone and he has the capacity to transform everyone.

Paul's final comment brings him back to where he began at the start of this section, speaking about his own ministry: 'For this I toil, struggling with all his energy that he powerfully works within me' (1:29). His very life and work are living testimony to the transforming grace and power of Christ. His energy and skill as a preacher of the gospel were not merely the transfer of the natural energy and abilities that used to be his as a Pharisee to what he now was as a Christian minister, but nothing less than the supernatural power and gifting of the Lord Jesus Christ himself.

One of the glories of the gospel is its ability to take people who are nothing in themselves and equip and enable them to become something and do things for God. It brings about a new focus and transformation of life that can only be explained as coming from a life that is now bound up with Christ.

7

The Goal of Faithful Ministry

For I want you to know how great a struggle I have for you and for those at Laodicea and for all who have not seen me face to face, ²that their hearts may be encouraged, being knit together in love, to reach all the riches of full assurance of understanding and the knowledge of God's mystery, which is Christ, ³in whom are hidden all the treasures of wisdom and knowledge. ⁴I say this in order that no one may delude you with plausible arguments. ⁵For though I am absent in body, yet I am with you in spirit, rejoicing to see your good order and the firmness of your faith in Christ. (Col. 2:1-5)

Although these verses take us to the beginning of a new chapter in Paul's letter, they are still very much the continuation of what the apostle has been saying in the previous verses as he gives further insight into what makes his ministry tick. However, his focus now is to help his readers see where its goals lie: what he is seeking to achieve in the lives of those to whom he ministers.

Understanding the goals of any ministry is an important part of evaluating its worth. Paul has no hesitation about warning his readers in Colossae that they are being 'deluded' by those who have quietly crept in among them and he unashamedly holds up the goals of what he is doing as a point of comparison.

Whereas it is perhaps easy to point to extreme examples of religious delusion in the form of various sects and cults that are forever popping up in the name of Christianity, there are other more subtle forms that appear that can be just as damaging to those who are taken in by them. There has been no shortage of Christian preachers and leaders who have charismatic personalities, who use their 'ministry' to build their own personal empire in one way or another. And that frequently involves them using their gifts to manipulate and control their followers without their realizing what is happening.

So to ask the question, 'Where is this leading?' in relation to anything that purports to be a Christian ministry, is a simple but effective way of getting to its heart. As Paul allows his own ministry to be tested in that way by the Colossians, it says a great deal not just about him, but also about those who were his rivals.

UNDERSTANDING THE DYNAMICS OF FAITHFUL MINISTRY

It is not without significance that for the third time in a few short verses Paul refers to the intensity of the 'struggles' and sufferings he has had to endure in order to fulfil his calling as a preacher of the gospel. We have already commented on that in part in the last chapter, but since it crops up again here in verse one, it invites some further thought.

We have said already that Paul has adopted an approach in handling the Colossian problem which is quite different from the way he handles the problems in other New Testament churches. In Galatia and Corinth, for example, he is very direct and explicit in the way he identifies what the specific issues troubling the church are – even to the point of publicly identifying the groups or individuals who were causing them. His approach in Colossae is quite different and we are in many ways left trying to 'read between the lines' to piece together what the Colossian problem actually was. But when we appreciate the pastoral wisdom and sensitivity bound up with Paul's approach, it is perhaps a little easier to make sense of what is going on and the kind of issues he is addressing.

If we assume that the new teachers who were influencing these relatively new believers in Colossae had already won the admiration and affection of their hearers through their message and ministry, any direct criticism of them by Paul was almost certain to be counter-productive, so he needed to approach the issue from a different angle.

A friend of mine in the ministry once faced a not dissimilar situation as he sought to minister to people who were very much in the grip of a serious distortion of the gospel, but who were deeply attached to those who had taught it to them. Amazingly my ministerial friend saw many of these people delivered from the false gospel they had believed without ever having to either directly criticize those who taught it, or challenge the most controversial details of what they were teaching. When I asked my friend how he managed to do that without an explosion of acrimony, he simply said, 'If you want to show a line is crooked, just draw a straight line beside it!' And that is precisely what Paul is doing here.

So when we pick up little details in the way Paul delivers his message that, by way of repetition and other devices, stress the straightness of his message, we have good reason to infer where the crookedness of his counterparts' teaching actually lies.

As Paul draws attention to the suffering he endured in his ministry and the suffering he says elsewhere is integral to genuine Christian discipleship, there is every reason to infer that the false teachers in Corinth were offering a pain-free variety of Christianity that was not Christianity at all. Indeed, given the apostle's repeated references to 'fullness', 'completeness' and 'riches' we begin to see them as an early example of the 'Come to Jesus and all will be well' type ministries that have attracted many followers over the years, but have ended up advancing the cause of the preacher and not that of Christ.

The fact that Paul says he endures these struggles not just for the sake of the Colossians, but 'for those at Laodicea and for all who have not seen me face to face' as well points to this whole dimension of ministry as being one of its authenticating features – one that is common to all true apostolic ministry.

Paul urges his readers to look hard at the dynamics of the ministries to which they might be drawn and ask themselves whether they are self-serving, or self-sacrificing for the sake of Christ.

REALIZING BLESSINGS ARE FOUND IN RELATIONSHIP

In the next two verses of this chapter Paul continues to tease out his exploration of the goals and objectives behind the ministry of those who were leaving their mark on the Colossian church by setting them over against the goals and objectives of his own ministry. And he does so by extending that 'straight line' we mentioned a moment ago. In this case his focus is on the blessings and benefits offered in the two different messages to which these Christians were being exposed.

Once again we can't help but notice Paul's shrewdness in the way he handles what is happening in Colossae. He spells out the benefits and blessings of salvation using language that he knew would resonate with what had been promised by the other teachers in that church, but then points to where and how these blessings can be found. The fact that he shifts his focus of reference at this point to go beyond the needs of the Christians in Colossae to include those in Laodicea and indeed all who have never met the apostle in person makes it clear that these are universal needs that are universally addressed in the gospel.

What are these needs? 'That their hearts may be encouraged, being knit together in love, to reach all the riches of full assurance of understanding and the knowledge of God's mystery, which is Christ, in whom are hidden all the treasures of wisdom and knowledge' (2:2-3).

Each of these is a deeply rooted need of the human heart and of our shared life as human beings. We all yearn for heartfelt encouragement, loving unity in our various webs of relationship and a reasonable measure of certainty in our understanding, knowledge and wisdom – especially when it comes to how we relate to God. To describe three of them, at least, as 'treasures' is no understatement on Paul's part: their value goes far beyond many other things we count as blessings in life and most definitely need to be pursued. But the burning question is where and how they can be found.

Once again Paul uses language that echoes the buzz words being used by the new breed of preacher who had surfaced in this church. In so doing he was not questioning the need for these things in life, but rather the way they were being defined and, more significantly, where they are to be found. We see that where he says that they are all not only defined by Christ but are actually found in relationship with him.

In a strange way it echoes one of the most serious shifts that has taken place in Western culture in centuries, namely the sexual revolution that began in the 1960s. An entire generation at that time decided to throw off what they saw as moral shackles which hindered their enjoyment of sexual intimacy. The belief that sex

belongs within marriage was seen as outdated and therefore dis-
pensable. Instead it was thought that what had previously been
seen as a rich and deep benefit of marriage could be enjoyed without needing the relationship of marriage. The ensuing fifty years
of sexual brokenness and scarred lives and hearts have told their
own sad story of how this really is not true.

The Christians in Colossae and many others like them have
been seduced with the notion that we can somehow have the rich
and deep benefits of intimacy with God without actually having
the relationship with God in which alone they flourish. The Bible
repeatedly describes the relationship between God and his people
as being a spiritual marriage where the deepest blessings of salvation derive from having our estrangement from him exchanged
for extraordinary intimacy with him. We cannot have the benefits
without the relationship and the only way to both find and sustain
that relationship is 'in Christ'. When Christ is somehow marginalized in our preaching and in our worship, the joys and blessings of
salvation very quickly disappear.

APPRECIATING THE PROTECTIVE ELEMENT IN MINISTRY

Paul knew full well that his words would already be jarring with his
hearers in this little congregation. By now they would be waking up
to the fact he was calling their newfound instructors and mentors
in the faith into question. So here he breaks cover, so to speak, and
tells his audience directly why he is writing in this way: 'I say this in
order that no one may delude you with plausible arguments' (2:4).

He does not mince his words. No matter how convincing this
new message may have sounded, it was deceptive and dangerous.
The hearers were being so swept away by the power of communication that they were utterly oblivious to the fine print in the
content of what they were hearing.

In many ways the red flag Paul was raising almost 2,000 years
ago has become one of the defining issues in the delusion that has
been sweeping through the entire world since the dawn of the age
of mass communication. There is no generation more skilled in
the techniques and technology of communication, yet none that is
less equipped to evaluate what is heard than the one of which we

[51]

are a part. It is hardly surprising, therefore, that it is our generation that has felt so misguided by politicians, financiers and, yes, by religious leaders as never before. The slick methods used to get 'the message' across have too often served to empty 'the message' of any meaningful content.

Just as Paul in his day was prepared to be blunt and outspoken in order to protect his hearers from delusion – especially in the area of life where they were most vulnerable – so today all who are serious about offering the hope of salvation to the world should be concerned to protect people from deception. That can only happen when the content of the message is kept true to the Christ from whom it comes.

ORDER AND STABILITY AS THE OUTCOME OF MINISTRY

However much Paul may have shocked his readers in the bluntness of what he has just said, he quickly tempers it with the words of reassurance found at the end of this section. 'For though I am absent in body, yet I am with you in spirit, rejoicing to see your good order and the firmness of your faith in Christ' (2:5).

Much and all as he would have preferred to be face to face with them having this conversation, he is absent from them; but such is the intensity of his pastoral concern he assures them that he is very much with them in spirit. He is not some detached and theoretical pontificator, but, even though he has never met them personally, is passionate about the fact they are one in spirit by virtue of their being one in Christ.

As he speaks to these people within the amazing closeness of relationship that is found in Christ, he wants them to know that he is not calling their profession of faith into question. Far from it, he is filled with joy to see how, despite the teachings they were being exposed to, they have not been shaken or plunged into confusion and disarray in their faith.

In reassuring them with these words, his intent is to quietly reaffirm the only safe foundation of their faith and heartbeat of their religion as being Christ himself.

8

The Heart and Soul of Genuine Faith

Therefore, as you received Christ Jesus the Lord, so walk in him,
⁷ rooted and built up in him and established in the faith, just as you
were taught, abounding in thanksgiving. ⁸ See to it that no one takes
you captive by philosophy and empty deceit, according to human tra-
dition, according to the elemental spirits of the world, and not accord-
ing to Christ. ⁹ For in him the whole fullness of deity dwells bodily,
¹⁰ and you have been filled in him, who is the head of all rule and
authority. (Col. 2.6-10)

Having just restated his confidence in the genuineness of the
Colossians' faith in Christ, Paul goes on to map out the shape
and contours of what such faith is and is not, once more narrowing
their focus to Christ and the uniqueness of who he is.

It would have been easy in one sense to simply allow his affir-
mation of these people's faith to rest with that; but, once more
reflecting the pastoral insight and concern that characterized the
apostle, he uses this as an opportunity to strengthen their grasp of
the faith. Learning to tell the difference between what is real and
what is counterfeit is a hard, but a vital lesson we need to learn
about life in general. (How easy it is to be conned into buying
something that is not the genuine article simply because we don't
know how to tell what is real and what is fake!) How much more –
and how much more serious – is our need to distinguish true from
false with something that has eternal implications and can mean
the difference between everlasting gain and everlasting loss.

The church in Colossae was being quietly taken over by a
mutant strain of Christianity, one that was ultimately doomed to
perish because it was, quite simply, not the real thing. Church history is littered with the corpses of countless such mutations of the
faith each of which caused a stir of excitement in their day, but

quickly died away because they were more about man than about God (leaving untold spiritual collateral damage in their wake) and many more continue to arise almost by the week. So the issues Paul spells out in terms of how we are to recognize the heart and soul of genuine faith could not be more pertinent.

GO ON IN THE FAITH IN THE WAY YOU BEGAN

Paul says, 'Therefore, as you received Christ Jesus the Lord, so walk in him…' (2:6). The 'therefore' clearly signals a connection with what he has been talking about in the previous verse. That is, his conviction that these Colossian Christians are indeed genuine believers. But, as we have already indicated, he is not content to leave it with a bare expression of his personal opinion. Even though he was an apostle, Paul knew that it was not for him in some priestly fashion to make definitive pronouncements on those who were truly saved and those who were not. Rather, he knew that the only way to prove the genuineness of faith is to see it being proved over time and under all kinds of testing circumstances. As Dr J. I. Packer has wisely said, the only way for a person to show that he or she is really converted is through their convertedness. Or, to use the language of an older generation of Christians, the Puritans, to see it displayed in 'the marks of grace' in a person's life. The Christian life is nothing more or less than the outworking of true Christian conversion and all that it entails.

That is why Paul highlights for his listeners the link between how they began in the faith and how they will go on and, in so doing, he challenges the false teachers who were suggesting that the Christian faith begins in one way, but goes on by some other means.

That disjunction between how faith begins and how it progresses has been all too common in the distortions of the Christian faith. From the 'start by faith, but go on by works' idea that surfaced in the Galatian churches to the 'start with Christ, but go on by the Spirit (through some secondary conversion)' which has become prevalent in more recent times, the implication has been that Christ is not enough.

Paul could not be more forceful in the way he reacts against such notions. Salvation began for these Colossians when they 'received

Christ' and the only way it could be worked out in their lives would be as they 'walk in him' (2:6). Several details are worth noting in the way Paul expresses himself in this verse.

The first is that he refers to the Saviour as, 'Christ Jesus the Lord'. At first sight there might not seem anything unusual about that designation, except that this is the only place in the New Testament where this combination of names and titles appears in this order. Linked to this is the fact that he says these believers 'received' him as such. The designation Paul gives to Jesus makes a penetrating statement about his authority as God's 'anointed one' and the uniqueness of his Person as God and man in human flesh – both of which are not only true in themselves, but are essential to the Saviour who is proclaimed in the gospel. So, when Paul says that the Colossians 'received' this Christ, it was not because they had physically met him in person, but had trusted in him as he had been presented to them as the Christ of the gospel record. (Unlike the 'Christ' who was now being presented in the new forms of teaching they were hearing.) There can only be one Christ who is authentic for faith from its beginning to its end and that is the one to whom the apostolic gospel bears witness.

The second detail to notice is Paul's call to 'walk in him' – not 'with him', but 'in him'. Again what may seem like a fairly insignificant detail is actually hugely important. It reminds us that salvation in all its fullness is never merely a co-operative venture between Christ and the Christian, but an ongoing relationship of our total dependence on him. Paul has already alluded to this with reference to his own life of faith and the way that it is the power of Christ that empowers his life (1:29). Such is the depth of this saving union that as these believers walked in union and communion with Christ in this way, they would be 'rooted and built up in him and established in the faith'. Paul's mixing of metaphors here only serves to strengthen the threefold image he is portraying of deeply-rooted spiritual vitality, leading to their being built up into the spiritual edifice that would be firm and secure at all times. The key to all three being not just 'faith', but 'the faith' in the sense of the body of teaching in the Bible that defines what salvation is and from whom it comes.

There was nothing novel or innovative in what Paul was saying in this: it was all 'as you were taught'. In other words, the message of Christ that had brought these people to faith and salvation was the same message of the same Christ who would bring them to the fulfillment of their faith and salvation. Hence the final qualifier in this verse: 'Abounding in thanksgiving'. The more they came to appreciate the depth and richness of the gospel and the more they came to prove it daily in their lives as they lived by faith in that gospel, the more they would be filled with wonder, love and praise for the God of the gospel and all he gives through his Son.

The gospel that we so often see as 'simple' never ceases to amaze us not just in the depth and scope of its content, but its promises and power to sustain all those who not only trust it, but dare to keep on trusting, come what may.

BE ON GUARD AGAINST ANYTHING THAT RIVALS CHRIST

It is that challenge to keep on trusting and keep on going in the way of the gospel that leads Paul into his next comment which is the negative counterpart to what he has just been saying. 'See to it that no one takes you captive by philosophy and empty deceit, according to human tradition, according to the elemental spirits of the world, and not according to Christ' (2:8).

He uses a word for 'see' that carries the sense of being on the lookout for something: knowing that there are threats and dangers lurking out there and being watchful against them. Except that in the case of the Colossians, these dangers were no longer just 'out there', they were very much 'in here' within the precincts of their own church. The need for vigilance in terms of what we accept as 'truth' in relation to faith and life cannot be stressed too much.

The seriousness of Paul's exhortation for these believers to be on guard is seen in the fact that he couples it with the threat of being 'taken captive'. The threat is far more than some minor divergence of opinion, or inconvenience to fellowship; but nothing less than a loss of freedom. It is no accident that it is rarely blatant heresy that leads people astray, but rather subtle distortions of basic Bible truths that lead to not-so-subtle distortion of its message.

Paul identifies how those distortions are introduced and the tell-tale signs of what they really are and how to recognize them. The vehicles by which they are carried are 'philosophy and empty deceit' or, as it might also be rendered, 'hollow and deceptive philosophy'. Paul was not for a moment writing off the idea or discipline of philosophy in general as being wrong. (Everyone is a philosopher whether they realize it or not.) Rather, he was warning against all attempts to make sense of the world and life without reference to God's truth revealed in his Word. Or, to put a sharper edge to it, even any attempt to do so in the name of Christianity in which human reason is not in submission to God's revelation.

What he means becomes clearer in what follows. Such empty and deceptive ideas about life are 'according to human tradition, according to the elemental spirits of the world, and not according to Christ'. The danger of the 'tradition' he mentions lies in the fact that it is 'human' in its origin. The Bible commends and indeed requires a God-approved tradition, or 'handing down from generation to generation' of those truths he has revealed – seen in Paul's instructions to Timothy (*2 Tim.* 2:2) – but it roundly challenges the kind of tradition that is merely manmade (*Mark* 7:8). We often think of such 'tradition' as being ideas and practices from bygone generations that hold the church hostage in the present; but ironically it can be equally true that the latest ideas and fashions to enter the church hold Christians to ransom, because they have come from men and not God.

Paul also points to 'the elemental spirits of the world' as another controlling factor in these dangerous philosophies that infiltrate and infect the family of God. There has been significant discussion and debate as to what Paul is seeking to convey by this expression, not least because it carries a range of possible meanings. Without getting into all the possibilities, it would seem the most likely one is a view of the physical world and the spirit world which saw the physical world being very much at the mercy of angels and demons. This view was common at that time and seems to have been a component of the new ideas that were entering the Colossian church: just a few verses later Paul has to warn his readers against an undue fixation with angels (2:18). His concern is not to dismiss or deny the existence or influence of such beings, but rather to avoid seeing them as some kind of independent powers without reference to God.

The biggest clue, however, to recognizing when faith is losing its way is when it is no longer 'according to Christ' – the Christ, as we have seen, who is revealed in the gospel. When he ceases to be at the heart of the message we believe, the key to the salvation in which we hope and the one who shapes the life of faith, then whatever our 'faith' may be, it is no longer worthy of being called 'Christian'.

NEVER LOSE SIGHT OF WHY CHRIST IS THE SOURCE

Paul brings us back yet again to the centrality of Christ and why it matters in the next two verses: 'For in him the whole fullness of deity dwells bodily, and you have been filled in him, who is the head of all rule and authority' (2:9-10).

There is one thing that sets Christ apart from anyone and anything else that people have looked to for life and salvation and it is the fact that he not merely claimed to be, but was seen to be the one in whom the fullness of deity dwelled in bodily form. He was both fully God and fully man. It is highly significant that Jesus did not placard that claim through any form of self-advertisement; he let his character, words and works speak for themselves. Indeed, in a most extraordinary way it was his death that voiced that claim most powerfully, as witnessed by the testimony of the commanding officer of the execution squad who oversaw the crucifixion (*Mark* 15:39).

Once more turning his deliberate choice of words to the specific situation faced by the Colossians, Paul reminds them that it is with him and with his fullness that they have been 'filled'. And in a thinly veiled jibe at the lesser spirit beings to whom these believers had been drawn he says that the authority and headship of Christ tower over whatever little power and authority they might wield.

Paul's pastoral logic could not be more compelling. If the infinite and absolute fullness of God who is supreme is concentrated and revealed in the Person of Christ then there simply is no-one or nothing else who can even come close to what he alone can give. He is not only the source of life; he is the only source of our salvation.

9

The Legal and Living Components of Salvation

In him also you were circumcised with a circumcision made with-
out hands, by putting off the body of the flesh, by the circumcision
of Christ, ^{12} having been buried with him in baptism, in which you
were also raised with him through faith in the powerful working of
God, who raised him from the dead. ^{13} And you, who were dead in
your trespasses and the uncircumcision of your flesh, God made alive
together with him, having forgiven us all our trespasses, ^{14} by cancel-
ling the record of debt that stood against us with its legal demands.
This he set aside, nailing it to the cross. ^{15} He disarmed the rulers and
authorities and put them to open shame, by triumphing over them in
him. (Col. 2:11-15)

One of the disadvantages in reading someone else's letters – especially if they belong to a time and place that are far removed from our own – is understanding why specific details are included and why certain things are expressed in a particular way. That sense of puzzlement surrounds at least the first two of the verses in this section and we will come to look more closely at it in a moment.

What is clear, however, is that Paul is continuing to build on what he has been saying, especially in relation to what constitutes genuine Christian faith and experience. The 'in him also...' that introduces the section links back into what the apostle has just said about the uniqueness of Christ in his Person and allows him to shift his focus to the uniqueness of Christ in his work.

The flow of Paul's reasoning is designed to take his readers from the objective truth of who Christ is and what he has done to the subjective difference it has made in their lives through their faith in the gospel. His approach is no different from the way he opens up the gospel in his other letters, reminding not just the Colossians, but all his readers that our personal experience of salvation does not have its roots in our private and personal experience, but in a unique person and unique events that took place at a specific point in space and time.

It is only as we keep that larger frame of reference in view that we will begin to grasp where Paul is going as his message unfolds and, more specifically, how it impacts our lives. As he opens up the salvation promised to us in the gospel more fully, he wants us to see its two crucial component parts: one that deals with our legal standing before God and the other our spiritual state.

SALVATION IN PICTURE FORM

The conundrum in this passage we alluded to at the start of this chapter relates to the reference to circumcision that seems to appear right out of the blue. So the question naturally arises as to what lay behind it and what Paul was seeking to address as he speaks of it.

Paul clearly had the Jewish rite of circumcision in mind as opposed to the other forms of circumcision that were practised in the ancient world, because he links it directly to Christ as the one in whom it finds its fulfillment. But how did this Old Testament rite come to be an issue in the Colossian church which, so far as we can tell, was made up largely of people who had come to faith from a non-Jewish background?

The answer in part at least lies with the historical detail from Josephus, mentioned in the Introduction, which pointed to some two thousand Jews being brought into this region by Antiochus III from Mesopotamia and Babylon in the early part of the second century B.C. Although it is hard to know whether or not there was still a Jewish community in Colossae, or to what extent the influences of Judaism lingered on in that locality, it would seem reasonable to assume that some form of Jewish ritual was still around. The fact that Paul speaks here of circumcision and further down of food laws and ceremonial and Sabbath days only serves to strengthen that assumption.

Whatever the precise reason may have been, the Colossian Christians, or some of them at least, were being exposed to the rite of circumcision in a way that was confusing their understanding of their faith and Paul seeks here to clarify it for them and help them to see it in the larger context of the message of salvation in the gospel.

What is clear is that in speaking of circumcision and baptism in the same sentence and linking them both to the death of Christ, the apostle was showing how both were given by God to be symbolic pictures of what is involved in salvation – one from an Old Testament angle and the other from the New. Neither rite in and of itself was able to bring about salvation, but both were linked in a special way by God to Christ as the one who alone would make the pictures become spiritual reality.

If we try and piece together the clues of what was happening among the Colossian Christians, it would seem that many, if not all of them, had not actually been circumcised. That seems to be the inference behind Paul's talking about 'the uncircumcision' of their flesh further down (2:13). But in telling them that they were already 'circumcised with a circumcision made without hands' (2:11), it sounds as though the apostle is responding to pressure being placed on them to receive this rite physically by telling them that all it signified had already been fulfilled when they had come to faith in Christ.

If that is accurate reconstruction of their situation, then the new influences that were affecting the church included an expectation that Christian males should be circumcised. And, given the mix of religious ideas and practices that was prevalent in that region at that time, that expectation was likely to be coming from a synthesis of Jewish and pagan religious ideas and practices as they infiltrated the church.

Paul's desire in all this is to show that the Old Testament rite of circumcision, which was the sign of the Covenant between God and his people and was linked to salvation (*Gen.* 17:1-14), was a graphic symbol of the removal of the sin and guilt that separates people from God. But it was only a symbol. The reality to which it pointed was found in what Paul here calls 'the circumcision of Christ' (2:11). This could either refer to Christ's death as a 'circumcision' or to the saving effectiveness of his death being applied to someone's heart when they come to faith. (It may well be the case that Paul has both in view.) But it is the way Paul links this reality to baptism that serves to reinforce the point he is making. Baptism was the New Testament rite, ordinance or sacrament that pointed to the same spiritual reality, but from the other side of the cross. Instead of a bloody ritual that depicted sin as being 'cut away' – anticipating the bloody sacrifice that Jesus had to make – baptism portrayed it as being 'washed away' because no further sacrifice was needed. More than that, as baptism in the New Testament is explained as having layers of significance which include Spirit baptism (*Titus* 3:5) and being joined to Jesus in his death, burial and resurrection (*Rom.* 6:1-11), Paul points here to the life-giving element of salvation to which baptism points.

In effect what Paul is doing in these verses is to reach into the murky and bloodied waters of ritualism that were confusing these Christians in Colossae to rescue two great God-given pictures that were being distorted to show that both circumcision and baptism point to the same glorious reality of new life and salvation that are found in Christ alone.

SALVATION IN ITS TWO PARTS

Without pausing for breath in what he is doing, Paul presses his point home further with his audience as he speaks of how the salvation Christ provides more than fully deals with the depth of our need as human beings in our sin. He demonstrates succinctly, but eloquently how Christ meets our twofold need.

In the first place he says, 'And you, who were dead in your trespasses and the uncircumcision of your flesh, God made alive together with him' (2:13). The thrust of this declaration is that those who once were spiritually dead have now, by virtue of their new relationship with Jesus Christ, been made alive. And this new life they receive in Christ is bound up with the fact that God raised him from the dead.

In that sense Paul is reminding us that our fundamental problem of being spiritually dead is met and answered through the resurrection of Christ. However, as we look carefully at what the apostle says, that does not happen through the resurrection in isolation. It is not as though God can somehow separate what we might call the living component of salvation from its underlying legal counterpart. Our lack of spiritual life as human beings is inseparably

[62]

bound up with our legal liability before God. Death is the penalty for sin and it is only when sin has been dealt with that the death sentence can be lifted.

That brings us to the second part in what Paul sets out as being necessary for salvation: '…having forgiven us all our trespasses, by cancelling the record of debt that stood against us with its legal demands' (2:13-14). Having spoken of our need of spiritual life, he now speaks of our need of legal pardon before the court of heaven.

The Colossian Christians to whom Paul was writing were only too conscious that even though they had come to Christ for salvation, they still struggled with sin and failure in their lives each day. They had yet to grasp the full weight of the salvation Christ has provided and so were wide open to the influences of false teachers who were saying they needed some additional measures to take them to a deeper level of peace of conscience and spiritual experience. In this case, it was the claim that they needed to undergo circumcision as an additional rite that would somehow serve to purify them more fully.

Paul makes it clear that there is nothing extra that Christians can contribute in order to put things right between them and God. Using past tenses in his verbs in this sentence, he makes it clear that all the sins and all the legal liabilities of those who come to faith in Christ have already been dealt with and they are free. 'The record of debt that stood against us with all its legal demands' has been 'cancelled'.

This is something every Christian needs to grasp. All too often we find ourselves being haunted by and even held hostage to our sins and failures from the past. Indeed Satan (whose name means 'accuser') delights in dredging up those shameful memories from the past, but what he never does is to remind us that Jesus has dealt with our past. The 'debt' we owed to God – a debt we could never begin to pay – now has 'cancelled' stamped across it in red! But where and when did this transaction take place?

THE CROSS AS THE KEY TO SALVATION

Paul's concern as he teases out this line of reasoning is to point the Colossians away from merely focusing on themselves and their own experience of salvation in a subjective sense. Although there was and is a vital place for such focus, it can never provide a secure foundation for the hope of salvation, because every Christian's experience of salvation is coloured by his or her daily struggle with sin. So here Paul takes his readers beyond what had happened and was happening in their lives individually to what had been done for them once and for all by Christ.

He explains to them that all this is bound up with what happened on the cross. 'This he set aside, nailing it to the cross' (2:14). The bad 'record' that haunted these Christians in Colossae had actually been dealt with on the day that Jesus died. Paul uses language that would have been familiar to his audience who were well aware of the details of crucifixion as an approved form of execution in the Roman world. It was the custom when this sentence was carried out that the 'charge sheet' of the crimes for which the condemned person was being put to death would be literally nailed to the cross above their head. Except that as the apostle uses that imagery in relation to Christians, the charge sheet of our crimes against God was nailed to someone else's cross and our penalty borne in his name and not our own.

It is not hard to see how the cross provides the key to dealing with our legal standing before God. We who once were rightly under condemnation before him as the Judge of all the earth can be justly pardoned and accepted on account of all that Christ accomplished there. But in what sense does the cross relate to our being 'made alive' with Christ?

Elsewhere Paul makes a clear connection between the physical resurrection of Jesus and the spiritual resurrection that takes place when a person becomes a Christian (*Eph.* 2:4-6), but he homes in on another dimension to that resurrection here, one that is also found in the cross and what Christ accomplished there.

The explanation for this lies in the fact that new life for God's people was not secured through what happened on Easter Sunday morning, but through what happened on Good Friday. That is true not merely because Christ could not have risen from the dead if he had not died in the first place; but rather, the ultimate cause of death would not have been dealt with if he had not died.

The cry of victory that we hear from Jesus' lips is not heard as he emerges from the tomb to the brightness of a new day; but from the darkness of cross in the moments before he died. Hence the closing statement in this passage: 'He disarmed the rulers and authorities and put them to open shame, by triumphing over them in him' (2:15).

It was through all he accomplished on the cross that Jesus secured the victory of the ages, indeed the victory that would secure eternity for all his people. Not only would it mean forgiveness for their sins and their guilty record being expunged, but it also signalled the death of death itself. By dealing with sin which is the cause of death, Jesus disarmed death of its destructive power and set his people free from its control. The proof that this really was so came three days later when he himself rose bodily from the grave.

However, there was more to it again. In a way that would resonate with the troubling new ideas that were swirling around the church in Colossae – ideas that had an unhealthy fixation with the unseen powers and rulers of the spirit world – Paul makes it clear that on the cross these threats to our peace and security have been dealt with as well. Using military imagery that would have been familiar to the people of his day, he paints the picture of an army parading through its hometown in a triumphal procession after a great victory. At the end of the procession would have come the defeated enemy prisoners of war: paraded in order to humiliate them.

When Jesus died on the cross it was not merely that the earthly authorities of the day conspired to humiliate and destroy him, but as is clear from the gospel record, the powers of darkness itself were the architects of that conspiracy. Little did they know that there was a higher plan and power at work and that God himself had chosen to use that very cross to seal their fate for eternity. The cross that they had intended for the humiliation of God has become the emblem of their defeat and shame.

10

The Key to Spiritual Growth and Progress

*Therefore let no one pass judgment on you in questions of food and drink, or with regard to a festival or a new moon or a Sabbath.
17 These are a shadow of the things to come, but the substance belongs to Christ. 18 Let no one disqualify you, insisting on asceticism and worship of angels, going on in detail about visions, puffed up without reason by his sensuous mind, 19 and not holding fast to the Head, from whom the whole body, nourished and knit together through its joints and ligaments, grows with a growth that is from God.* (Col. 2:16-19)

Throughout this letter Paul has been responding to a situation where Christians who were still relatively young in the faith were being unsettled by incomers who questioned the message they had believed when they became Christians. Seeds of doubt were being sown in their minds as to whether or not what was offered in the gospel they had heard was enough. The apostle's response has been to counter the claim that their Christian experience was in some way deficient was by pointing again and again to the 'fullness' that not only resides in Christ because of who he is, but is promised in Christ to all who trust in him.

In the verses we looked at in the last chapter we saw how Paul highlights both aspects of that fullness, in order to guard his hearers against being deceived and taken captive by ideas that sounded plausible, but lacked any biblical foundation. He now goes on to bolster that argument with further warnings against the damage these new teachings would cause if the Colossian Christians blindly took them on board.

Although the language he uses in this section has something of a negative and defensive tone to it, Paul's purpose is entirely positive. Far from backing his readers into a corner, his intent is that they may be so strengthened in their faith that they would grow increasingly into healthy spiritual vitality and usefulness. It is only as they become aware of the kind of individuals and influences that impede such growth that they will be able to overcome such obstacles as were being placed in their way.

ISSUES THAT CAN HINDER SPIRITUAL GROWTH

The fact that Paul tells his Colossian readers 'let no one pass judgment on you' means that that is exactly what was happening to them and it was having a serious unsettling effect on them. Nobody likes to be criticized, but when it goes beyond that to feeling condemned it becomes a major hindrance to getting on with life. The language Paul uses here is strong language and it reflects the degree of pressure that was being placed on the believers in Colossae by those who had come in among them.

Even though Christians are meant to be discerning in what they believe and practise and exercise good judgment over who they follow, they are not to be judgmental. When that kind of spirit gets into a church it not only does serious damage to its internal fellowship among its people, it also becomes a major hindrance to the gospel and the way it is perceived by those outside the church. Yet that appears to have been what was happening in that church in Lycus Valley. The gospel was being reduced to a list of 'dos' and 'don'ts' and Paul was adamant that this should not happen, because when it does, it seriously hinders spiritual growth among God's people and limits their effectiveness as ambassadors for Christ.

It is worth pausing for a moment to see what kinds of issues were being used as excuses for such condemnation among the Colossians. Paul lists them as being, 'questions of food and drink, or with regard to a festival or a new moon or a Sabbath' (2:16) – in other words, food and drink regulations and requirements that were bound up with the weekly, monthly and yearly cycles of the religious calendar.

Even though such stipulations were a feature of many of the religions of the day, it is almost certain that in the case of the Colossians, they were coming from a Jewish quarter. The fact that Paul goes on to say, 'These are a shadow of the things to come' (2:17) could only be true in relation to Old Testament regulations and not their religious counterparts found in paganism and the syncretism of that region.

Whatever the source of these issues that were being raised, Paul says they were not to become defining issues either for the gospel or the church. As he says elsewhere: 'For the kingdom of God is not a matter of eating and drinking but of righteousness and peace and joy in the Holy Spirit' (*Rom.* 14:17).

Too often in the history of the church these kinds of things have surfaced and resurfaced as tests of orthodoxy among God's people. The genuineness of a person's profession of faith has been measured by their stance on drinking alcohol, or use of tobacco, or the company they keep. Or the faithfulness of a church gauged by its style of worship, or observance or otherwise of the high days and holy days of the Christian calendar. The reality is that since New Testament times there has been latitude on these matters. Individual Christians and churches have been free to reach their own conclusions on them in light of their own conscience as it is shaped by Scripture.

It is not these peripheral issues that distinguish between true and false churches and Christians and they are certainly never to be used as a means to pass judgment on either. The ultimate test of both is Christ and that is precisely where Paul is pointing his readers in what he says here.

The fact that he introduces this passage with the word 'therefore' points back to all he has said about Christ in terms of who he is and what he has done as the key to authentic Christianity. And because he has reaffirmed Christ as being the essence of the gospel and the sole focus of faith, he immediately rules out food, drink and the observance of holy days as being the test of true faith.

More than that, it is what the apostle goes on to say that is most significant: 'These are a shadow of the things to come, but the substance belongs to Christ' (2:17). He is clearly stating that all these dietary and calendar laws had their place in Old Testament, but it was only temporary. They were given by God at that stage of his dealings with his people to prepare them for and point them towards the coming of Christ as his promised Redeemer. God's intrusion into the most mundane aspects of their life – what they ate and how they used their time – was meant to foreshadow the fact that he would come in person through his Son as the one who is the Lord of life in its totality. Their salvation would be found and fulfillment of life enjoyed not through the observance of seemingly petty rules and regulations, but in living relationship with the Lord of all.

That statement in itself brings home the seriousness of what is at stake. Why settle for things that were only meant to be reflections of the good things to come when God wants us to enjoy the great reality that is found in Christ?

Perhaps the one thing that has become a source of significant debate in this passage among Christians is Paul's mention of 'a Sabbath' in the list of things for which the Colossians were not to allow themselves to feel condemned. Some have argued that the apostle was downplaying the place and importance of a day of rest in the life of the church and, indeed, its being good for the world. Whereas it is possible to get that interpretation out of this sentence when viewed narrowly, it is hard to square it with the immediate context, let alone the wider teaching of the Bible.

What Paul is condemning here is the misuse of Old Testament regulations: making them function in a way they were never meant to function. He was not addressing the wider question of how the principles contained in those regulations were meant to carry through into the life of the New Testament church.

The Sabbath principle runs too deep and extends too far in the message of Scripture for the idea of one day of the week being set apart as the day of rest for God's people to be dismissed in a part-sentence like this. We should be careful that we don't rush to wrong conclusions about what Paul is saying here in relation to the Sabbath day no longer having a place in the Christian church.

INDIVIDUALS WHO ARE OBSTACLES TO PROGRESS

At first glance the next verse in this passage seems to be just a variation on the two that have gone before, only this time with a slightly different focus, except that there is one little detail that should make us look more closely. It is the fact that Paul personalizes what he is talking about here. It is not just the particular influences themselves that should be a source of concern, but the individuals who lie behind them. So here he seems to have a particular person in mind when he speaks of 'no one' because he refers to 'his sensuous mind' at the end of the verse.

Issues make an impact on people's lives, but it is the individuals behind the issues that make an even deeper impact. And Paul points to the character and conduct of this particular individual in Colossae as sounding warning bells about there being something seriously wrong not only with him, but also with his message.

Another contrast between this verse and the two we have just considered is the fact that although Paul's concern in them was to highlight dangerous influences that were coming into the church from Judaism, here he highlights the threat from paganism. The references to asceticism, worship of angels and visions (2:18) are more likely to have come from the pagan mysticism of that region than from a purely Jewish source. But it is the linkage between the influences and the individual through whom they came that is both striking and significant.

The word that is translated 'asceticism' by the ESV carries the sense of excessive humility – the NIV renders it 'false humility'. It is the oxymoronic idea that such self-deprecation and self-denial are somehow a means of gaining virtue before God and in the eyes of others.

The 'worship of angels' is almost certainly a reference to praise and adoration being directed towards heavenly beings. (Some have suggested it could mean worship that is 'like that of the angels', which is possible, but not probable.) Given the fascination with the unseen world of spirits that permeated that part of Asia Minor, it is not hard to see how such practices may well have been creeping into the church in Colossae and that they were becoming a requirement for acceptable worship. Both the Old Testament and the New make it clear that worship is reserved exclusively for God and not for any of his creatures – not even those who belong to the heavenly realm. So even to suggest such a practice in the church, let alone insist upon it, was idolatrous.

The third thing that was being insisted upon that Paul names here is 'going on in detail about visions'. The way he phrases it puts the emphasis on things an individual has seen – so his concern is about supposed private and personal revelations from God. Even though in New Testament times God was still using dreams and visions as a means by which to make himself known, they were not the norm. Instead it was through the apostolic preaching of the Old Testament and the testimony of the apostles themselves that the final chapter of God's written revelation was being given. So for someone in Colossae to be insisting there should be more emphasis on visions was seriously out of step with what was shaping New Testament churches.

All three of these influences which Paul highlights carry the appearance of religious piety, but in a perverse way, instead of cultivating a genuine deeper devotion to God, they were becoming a serious distraction – drawing attention instead to the individuals who were caught up in these practices. It is perhaps surprising that there have always been displays of piety in the church that are more about man than about God. And one of these features of such displays is that they create the sense that those who have not experienced these things, or display them in their own lives, are somehow inferior to those who have. Paul still says we should not let anyone make us feel disqualified for these reasons.

It is, however, what Paul says about the unnamed someone at the end of this verse that is particularly damning. Despite the false humility he was promoting, he was 'puffed up without reason by his sensuous mind'. It was not just that he had a falsely inflated opinion of himself, but that his opinion was fueled by the self-gratifying appetites of the world.

Too often those who push hardest to introduce either legalistic requirements or quasi-mystical spirituality in churches, and insist that they are the hallmarks of genuine Christianity, are more interested in self-promotion than the glory of God and the good of his people. It is only when their character and priorities in life are seen for what they really are that the things they insist upon are exposed for what they are not.

THE KEY TO SPIRITUAL HEALTH AND VITALITY

The most positive statement that Paul makes in the midst of this is couched in a negative: 'and not holding fast to the Head, from whom the whole body, nourished and knit together through its joints and ligaments, grows with a growth that is from God' (2:19). The one thing that this particular individual and the false teachers generally in Colossae were neither advocating in their teaching nor doing themselves was the very thing that was absolutely necessary for real spiritual health and vitality. Given the force and weight of what Paul says in this brief statement, we would do well to explore it more fully.

The most important thing about the spiritual growth and vitality that Paul has in view here is that it is 'growth that is from God'. It is not from man, nor methods, programmes or practices; it comes from God himself. Paul has already alluded to this in his own personal experience when he spoke about the energy of Christ at work in him enabling him to keep going in the work of the ministry (1:29). Any growth of the church that is real must ultimately be the supernatural work of God in the hearts and lives of his people.

It is a growth that is founded in our being in union with Christ as 'the Head, from whom the whole body, nourished and knit together through its joints and ligaments, grows'. Again Paul has used this language earlier in the letter in a way that emphasized the vital connection that exists between the head and the body as a vivid metaphor of the profound relationship between Christ and his people (1:18). The apostle is merely echoing what Christ himself articulated using a different word picture of a vine and its branches (*John* 15:1-11).

The vigour and extent of this growth are bound up with 'holding fast to the Head'. Even though as Christians we are joined to Jesus in saving union with him, we nevertheless need to cultivate communion with him in terms of meaningful relationship as opposed to mere nominal attachment. Jesus distinguishes between these in his discourse in John's Gospel in terms of branches which 'abide' or 'remain' in the vine as opposed to branches that only appear to be attached, but in reality are not: the presence or absence of fruit being the telltale sign of which is which.

However, what was arguably the most significant little detail in this verse for the Colossians in particular was the fact that through this relationship with Christ, 'the whole body, nourished and knit together through its joints and ligaments, grows'. Growth and vitality are not for an elite few who have been initiated into some spiritual inner circle. Paul is passionate about the corporate character of the Christian life. The idea of a Christianity that was merely private and personal would have been an alien concept to him and he knows only too well that the influences that were being brought to bear in Colossae were fragmenting the church there.

Arguably that same detail is one that needs to be most highlighted for many Christians and churches in our own day for whom the Christian faith is more about individual experience than a shared life as part of God's family. But perhaps that explains why spiritual growth and vitality are all too often absent for many who profess conversion.

The key to genuine spiritual wellbeing and usefulness is inseparably tied to our being bound up together as God's people in the same bundle of life with Christ. It is only as we 'hold on' to him as our living head that we will grow in fellowship with him and with one another as his people and know the joy of being useful to him as we serve the cause of his kingdom.

11

Joined to Jesus in His Death

*If with Christ you died to the elemental spirits of the world, why, as if
you were still alive in the world, do you submit to regulations –* [21] *'Do
not handle, Do not taste, Do not touch'* [22] *(referring to things that all
perish as they are used) – according to human precepts and teachings?*
[23] *These have indeed an appearance of wisdom in promoting self-made
religion and asceticism and severity to the body, but they are of no
value in stopping the indulgence of the flesh.* (Col. 2:20-23)

So far Paul has been spelling out the fundamental truths and
principles that underpin the new life a person has in Christ
when they come to faith. He has been contrasting them with the
distorted notions of the Christian life that have been infiltrating
the church in Colossae to show that what the false teachers are
claiming as the key to 'Christian' living is both unfounded and
unworkable. All the way through his letter he has been pointing to
Christ as the key and now he sets out to apply that truth practically
to the way these believers in Colossae were trying to live their life.

These verses lead us into the practical application of all the
apostle has been teaching up to this point and, as such, reflect the
pattern that Paul follows in many of his letters (and at the same
time give us a glimpse into the way his mind works). Just as a
building needs a solid foundation and a secure infrastructure or
framework to be put in place before its frontage and superstructure
can be erected, so it is in our lives individually as Christians and
corporately as the church. The foundations of who and what we
are as Christians are sunk deep into Jesus Christ in terms of who he
is and all that he has done for his people through the greatness of
salvation. He is the bedrock of our new existence: set free from an
old life in sin and brought into a whole new life in fellowship with

God. Rising directly out of that foundation is an intricate framework of truth and teaching provided in God's Word that spells out the component parts of the great salvation we have in Christ and the wherewithal he has given through his Word and Spirit to live it out in practice.

In other words, in all his letters Paul wants his readers to understand that what we are as Christians rests primarily on the truth and principles of the gospel – what God has done for us and given to us through his Son. The focus of faith must always be outside of ourselves and be in Christ as the source and substance of our salvation. That note needs to be sounded repeatedly in every generation because the instinct to focus faith either on ourselves and our own efforts to change, or else on some manmade formula, runs deep. That was certainly the situation the apostle was having to address here in Colossae.

So, as we reach this critical point in his letter, he moves from the groundwork he has been laying (which actually involved a significant amount of demolition of false teaching and uprooting of wrong ideas) to actually spelling out the difference it all makes in practice. Despite all that had been going wrong in this little church, he had never questioned for a moment the genuineness of these people's conversion; so now he sets out to encourage them to look more directly at who and what they are in Christ and live in the light of what that means.

In some ways it is not unlike the challenge a newlywed couple face as they begin married life together – especially if they have been used to being single for a long time. The temptation for them is to try to live their new life in marriage as if they were both still single but now just happen to live under the same roof and share the same bed. The truth they need to get their heads around is that they are not single any more. That through their union they have become joined in such a way that from now on each will shape the other. And the practicalities of that new mindset will work themselves out, not just in how they relate to each other, but in the way they live their own life in all its dimensions from that point onwards.

So here Paul starts to tease out the practicalities of what it means to be joined to Jesus in his death and how that will make the world of a difference to the way we live. In the next chapter he will develop that thought in terms of what it means to be joined to Jesus in his resurrection, but we will come to that later.

THE DIFFERENCE A DEATH MAKES

Death is, in its very essence, a defining moment in anyone's existence. When someone dies and leaves this world behind, they are no longer controlled by its powers and influences and no longer exposed to its liabilities. So there is a real sense in which death releases a person from the constraints they were under when they were alive. And that is the point Paul seeks to impress on his readers at this point.

He has already drawn attention to Christ's death and in particular to its never-ending implications for those who are joined to him through new birth and saving faith. He made reference to this explicitly in the first chapter of the letter where he says, 'And you who once were alienated and hostile in mind, doing evil deeds, he has now reconciled in his body of flesh by his death, in order to present you holy and blameless and above reproach before him, if indeed you continue in the faith ...' (1:21-23). He links the life of these Christians to the death of Jesus not merely in the sense that he has reconciled them to God through his sacrifice; but also in the sense that it becomes the life-transforming principle controlling their sanctification.

He then goes on to allude to Christ's death later on when he speaks of how we as Christians have been 'buried with him in baptism' (2:12). Here too Paul has the double-edged significance of the cross in view as the instrument of reconciliation in a once for all sense, but also as the means of dealing with sin in the outworking of the life of faith.

These strands of thought come together in a very pointed way as Paul puts his readers on the spot and says, 'If with Christ you died to the elemental spirits of the world, why, as if you were still alive to the world, do you submit to regulations ... ?' (2:20). By using the word 'if' at the beginning of this sentence, the apostle is not calling the genuineness of his readers' salvation into question, but rather pressing home its full significance. Translating it to read, 'Since you died with Christ ...' as other versions do, captures the sense more accurately.

[77]

His point is this. When these Colossians heard the gospel, were made alive by God's Holy Spirit and put their faith in Jesus Christ, at that moment in time they were brought into union with Christ in a way that joined them with every detail of what Christ had accomplished through his life, death, resurrection and exaltation in history. Even though they knew that was true in principle, they still needed to get their heads and hearts around what it meant for them in reality.

They were like that married couple we mentioned a moment ago who 'knew' they were married, but who were living in a way that robbed them of the full potential of their new relationship. They had failed to grasp the full implications of what Christ's death meant for them. Specifically, that it had not only paid the price for their sin, but it had also secured their release from what Paul earlier described as 'the domain of darkness' transferring them instead into 'the kingdom of his beloved Son' (1:13).

The specific reference to 'the elemental spirits' as that to which they had died is significant. Paul has already mentioned them towards the beginning of this chapter when he spoke of the Colossians as having been taken captive 'by philosophy and empty deceit according to human tradition, according to the elemental spirits of the world, and not according to Christ' (2:8). As we noted when we looked at that verse, Paul had in mind those unseen spiritual powers of the universe – angelic as much as demonic – that play out their influence in the life of the world. Having 'died' to their control and influence and been brought instead under the kingship of Christ they ought no longer to live as though they were at the mercy of their powers.

So his question to these Christians is this: 'If you no longer belong to the kingdom of this world, why are you living as if you do?' The powers and influences, rules and regulations to which these believers were subjecting themselves and which were being imposed on them had been rendered null and void by the death of Jesus because they had no ability in themselves to make anyone holy.

It is one of the greatest truths of the gospel, yet one of the hardest for Christians to really grasp. The instinct that makes us think that our acceptance with God and ability to please him somehow comes through keeping rules runs so deep in our hearts that it blinds us to the power of the cross to not only justify, but also sanctify us before God. So too, no matter how much we may know we have been released from the domain of darkness through the death of Christ, it is all too easy to live as though we had not. It is for that reason that Christians again and again lapse into varying forms of legalism on the one hand and spiritual fatalism on the other which stunt rather than encourage their growth in grace.

The death of Jesus makes the world of difference in the lives of all who put their hope and trust in him for their salvation. We can never go back to that truth too often.

WISDOM THAT'S WORTH LIVING BY

Paul develops this thought in more detail by challenging the kind of rules and regulations these people had been encouraged to embrace. Even though they are clearly appealing (why else would they have found a foothold in their lives?) they are fundamentally flawed. And the apostle pinpoints that flaw when he describes them as only having the 'appearance of wisdom' (2:23).

All too often the idea of 'wisdom' gets confused with that of 'knowledge'; but there is a vital distinction to be made between them. Knowledge is the accumulation of information, insights and understanding in life; wisdom is the ability to process them in a meaningful and practical way into how we actually live our lives. The word that is used for 'wisdom' in the Hebrew language and which crops up repeatedly in the Old Testament means 'skill for living' and that is very much what Paul has in view here.

There are many people whose heads are full of knowledge and ideas, but whose lives are far from God and in a mess and it was people like that who had infiltrated the church in Colossae and were damaging God's work in the lives of his people there. In short, theirs was the wisdom of the fallen world out of which these Colossian Christians had been rescued. A world which had contrived rules and regulations as a means to gaining God's favour and living a life that was pleasing to him, but which was still as far from God as ever. However attractive the 'appearance' of such wisdom may have been, it was useless when it came to dealing with man's deepest problem.

It is not without significance that Paul should flesh out that thought by pointing to the way it is expressed in 'religion'. Its appeal lies in the 'asceticism and severity to the body' that lies so very much at its heart. Part of the attraction of religion generally is the awareness shared by every human being is that we not only do bad things, but at our core we are actually bad people. And somewhere in our human psyche is the sense that our offence is not merely against our fellow men, but an unseen God to whom we must one day answer. Because sin is so bad we know it deserves punishment, so we think that if that punishment can be self-inflicted it will somehow take away the need for us to be punished by the One we have offended. It becomes the means of making atonement with God by our own means. In that sense, as Paul says, such religion really is 'self-made' and therefore ineffective before the God to whom it is offered.

That point is underscored in what has been said in the preceding verses about the specific kinds of regulations that were circulating among these people. It was not merely that they had to do with 'things that all perish as they are used', but also that they were merely based on 'human precepts and teachings' (2:22).

The wisdom of the world is simply not worth living by, not only because it is manmade as opposed to God-given, but more so because it is ineffective in producing the true and lasting life that we know we need. It is God's wisdom in the gospel that truly makes sense and that we so much need to know that we are at peace with God.

THE ONLY ANTIDOTE TO SIN

The specific aspect of that peace with God which Paul has in mind here is the peace of knowing not just that our sins have been forgiven and our guilt removed, but that we are actually making progress in our fight against temptation and in our efforts to live a life that is pleasing in God's sight. Hence the way he dismisses these quasi-religious expressions of worldly wisdom in Colossae as being 'of no value in stopping the indulgence of the flesh' (2:23). They are useless in themselves when it comes to rooting out corrupt thoughts in our minds, desires in our hearts and the words and deeds that flow from them in our lives.

Yet so many Christians find it hard to accept that this is indeed the case. They quite literally tie themselves up in knots with a tangled web of 'dos' and 'don'ts' as they try to live for God and seek the joy of his salvation. Except the further they go down this road, the less they know his nearness and the more miserable they become through their own hypocrisy and sense of failure.

The bottom line in what Paul is saying is that laws – religious or otherwise – can never in themselves make us better people. That is plain to see in the secular world as governments try to legislate their way towards a better life and more harmonious communities. No matter how many laws they put in place, or how severe may be the penalties that are attached to them, they are powerless in themselves to change people's lives. Such is the potency of what Paul here calls 'the flesh' – the spirit of rebellion in the human heart – that it takes something more powerful than law to deal with it. Human beings are hard-wired to indulge its rebellious instincts and gratify its desires (covertly or otherwise) that they require extraordinary measures to make a difference.

What, then, according to Paul does have 'value' when it comes to stopping these passions and urges that rise up within us. Interestingly it is not something extra or something new. (That is what the Colossians had been conned into thinking by the false teachers in their midst.) Rather, it was something that they already had: namely, their union with Christ in his death. The end of this paragraph takes us right back to where it began. Paul wants his Colossian hearers to go back to where the roots of their salvation lay. As they had been joined to Jesus in all that he is and all that he has done, so he alone is able to provide all they need for salvation and for starting to live the life to which God had called them.

So as he reminds them that they had been united with Christ in his death, he was pressing home the fact that through that death they were brought under his lordship in his kingdom and given the ability to actually deal with sin in their lives.

[81]

12

Joined to Jesus in His Resurrection

If then you have been raised with Christ, seek the things that are above, where Christ is, seated at the right hand of God. ² Set your minds on things that are above, not on things that are on earth. ³ For you have died, and your life is hidden with Christ in God. ⁴ When Christ who is your life appears, then you also will appear with him in glory. (Col. 3:1–4)

The chapter division that separates this section from the one that we have just looked at should not obscure the fact they are very much connected. The clue lies in the 'If' that introduces each paragraph and the 'with Christ' that is common to both. Paul is continuing to open up the significance of what it means for Christians to be joined to Jesus in two vital senses: in his death and in his resurrection.

This whole component of what it means to be a Christian is so important in Paul's teaching that he not only refers to it both directly and indirectly in many places, but he expounds it at some length in his letter to the Romans (6:1-14). What Jesus accomplished through his death and resurrection has a direct bearing not only on how a person becomes a Christian, but how they are enabled to go on to live the Christian life.

If the overall thrust of the preceding passage was to impress upon the Colossians the significance of Christ's death for them in terms of its marking a decisive break with the life they had known prior to their conversion, the main thrust in this section is to spell out the whole new life that they have begun as they are united with Christ in his resurrection.

RAISED WITH CHRIST

Even though Paul is clearly leading into a section of practical application in this chapter in which he calls on the Colossians to live out their Christian life in obedience to God's commands, it begins with yet another reminder of what God has done for us in Christ. It is his way of saying that God never tells his people to do anything for him without first reminding them of what he has done for them.

There is very good reason for his doing that. If it is true as Paul says elsewhere, that we by nature are 'dead in trespasses and sins' (*Eph.* 2:1), then no amount of commanding on God's part will lead to any kind of responding on ours. We are incapable of truly hearing, let alone obeying God's voice. More than that, left to our own devices, no amount of trying to please God on our part will even begin to bring about the restoration that we need in our relationship with him. God's Law by itself only serves to accentuate the depth of our fallenness in sin. But it is the mark of God's grace – his unmerited favour – that what we can never earn by our effort, he freely provides in his love. Paul wants us to know that it is not merely by grace that God saves us, but also by grace that we are enabled to live for him.

So, having already reminded the Colossians of how much God has provided for them through the death of Christ, he now turns his attention to what is theirs through his resurrection.

Once again he introduces this strand of teaching with the word 'if' in the same sense as before of 'since this is the case, then certain things can be expected to follow'. The focus this time is the fact that in their salvation they have not only died with Christ, but they have also been raised with him to a completely new life. He has already alluded to this in his opening prayer for the Colossians when he asked that God would strengthen them 'with all power' (1:11). This is the same concern that Paul had for himself as he pursued the life of faith. He expressed it elsewhere in terms of his longing to know Christ 'and the power of his resurrection' (*Phil.* 3:10). He knew that the ability that he and every Christian needed to live for God could only come from God himself through Jesus Christ.

So before the apostle confronts his readers with the challenges of the new life to which they had been called and as it affected the whole web of relationships they were in, he first brings them back to the one relationship that had literally made them new people: their relationship with Christ.

LONGING FOR A DIFFERENT WORLD

The first great practical implication of being 'raised with Christ' that Paul identifies is that as Christians we should now 'seek the things that are above' (3:1). The relevance of that for the believers in Colossae was plain to see. The teachers who had come into their midst were fostering an approach to faith that was more concerned with earthly rules and rituals than with heavenly things; and that was doing serious damage to their faith.

There are several significant thoughts embedded in what Paul is saying here. In the first place there is his reference to Christ's resurrection and what it means for Christians to be bound up with it in their new relationship with Christ. At one level, as we have hinted already, it points to the supernatural power that brought Jesus back to life from the dead as being precisely the same supernatural power that is needed to bring a sinner from spiritual death to new life in fellowship with him. When a person becomes a Christian it involves a supernatural act of God. However, at another level it points to the exaltation that Jesus underwent in his resurrection. In his death and burial Jesus experienced the terrible depths of humiliation that sin brings on a person. But God did not abandon him in that state; rather, he vindicated him by raising him from death and endorsed all it accomplished to the highest degree by giving him the place of greatest honour at his right hand.

In that sense, when someone is joined to Jesus in his resurrection, they not only share that God-given power that enables them to live a new life, but they also share in the exaltation of Christ. More than that, they now belong to and are destined for that place of glory in which he now reigns. If that is true, then we ought to be fixated by who we now are and where we are going because of him.

This would have come as a welcome reminder, if not a reassuring revelation, to these Colossian Christians who, as they listened to the novel teachings that were circulating in their church, were really coming to believe that there was something missing from their life. And since they were being encouraged to fill the void in their spiritual life by focusing on the earthly realm, only to be further frustrated, what a relief to hear Paul tell them they had been pointed in the wrong direction. Being bound up with Jesus in his resurrection, as much as with his death, gave them a whole new orientation of life.

As they were now already exalted with him and their eternal destiny bound up with him, then it stood to reason that he and the world to which he belongs should become their all-consuming passion. So Paul tells them, 'Seek the things that are above, where Christ is, seated at the right hand of God'. The word translated 'seek' carried overtones of longing or yearning for something – having a deep desire that controls the whole direction of life. An older translation rendered Paul's exhortation in this way: 'Set your affections on things above', using 'affections' with the sense of the inner disposition of life that governs the way a person lives.

The tense he chooses for the verb in this exhortation (a present active imperative) points to something that is both deliberate and ongoing. That is, the need to consciously nurture those longings of the heart by literally seeking the object of its desire, namely Christ.

That language echoes what is heard so often in the Psalms that speak of the deepest longings of the human heart that can only be satisfied by God himself: 'As the deer pants for the flowing streams, so pants my soul for you, O God. My soul thirsts for God, for the living God' (*Psa.* 42:1-2). We can never rest content until we are fully and finally with him.

It is strange that Christians and churches all too often preoccupy themselves with the earthly trappings of the Christian life rather than with Christ himself. They focus on buildings, programmes and forms of worship, rather than with the One who is our Saviour and the world to which he belongs. But because that is so often the case, it is not surprising that so many Christians and churches are unsettled and feel as though they are being short-changed because their desires have been misdirected.

YOUR MIND MATTERS

It is not without significance that Paul orders his exhortations at the beginning of this chapter in the way he does, speaking first of the disposition of our heart as Christians to then speaking of the focus of our thoughts. If he had reversed the order, then his gospel could be accused of being a religious version of mind-over-matter psychology; but that is not the case.

Having begun by reminding his readers of the great spiritual realities that are rooted in Christ and which are the basis of the transformation of life these believers have experienced, he goes on to speak about how that impacts their disposition of heart on the one hand, but also their mindset on the other. So he says emphatically, 'Set your minds on things above, where Christ is, seated in glory' (3:2).

As with the previous exhortation, the apostle uses the same verb form and tense that speaks of conscious and consistent action. There is nothing casual or careless about what he has in view here, but rather the need to re-order the whole way we think.

Paul expresses the same thought in Romans where he speaks about the far-reaching difference the gospel makes to those who embrace it. Having opened up the gospel in all its fullness in the first eleven chapters, he urges his readers, 'Do not be conformed to this world, but be transformed by the renewal of your mind' (12:2). It is only as our thought patterns are tuned to Christ and to the new creation order he has brought into being by his work of redemption that our lives in turn are brought into conformity with that new order to which we now belong.

The Colossians were feeding their minds on mystic and religious trivia served up by the false teachers who were wielding their influence among them and the effect of that was taking its toll on the fruitfulness and usefulness for which Paul had praised them in his opening prayer. So Paul strongly urges them – as with what he says in Romans, in view of the gospel realities – to learn to think about themselves and about life generally in light of Christ and all he has accomplished.

The fact he underscores his positive exhortation with a negative counterpart, 'not on things that are on earth', only serves to emphasize the seriousness of the point he is making. It is in our nature to understand ourselves and our life merely from the perspective of this world, forgetting that it is a fallen world; but if we are Christians, we actually belong to a different world and that new reality defines what we are.

Over the years my family and I have found ourselves living at times in different countries and in different cultures. One of the biggest challenges we have faced in so doing has been learning to think our way into those new situations into which we have come and to which, at least for those times, we have belonged. Paul is simply saying to us, as much as to the Colossians, 'Think your way in to what you have become and to where you now belong in Christ!'

WHERE DO WE NOW BELONG?

It is the issue of where we truly belong as Christians that forms the next thought Paul articulates in this section: 'For you have died and your life is hidden with Christ in God' (3:3). His repetition of the fact that in Christ we as Christians 'have died' is simply a reminder that our ties with this world have been decisively broken through our union with him in his death. To use the language of Jesus as he prays for his disciples, although we are 'in the world'; we are no longer 'of it' (*John* 17:11, 16). Even though in this present time this world is our 'home', in an ultimate sense it is not, because in Christ we belong somewhere else.

Paul's choice of words to identify where that 'somewhere else' actually is could hardly be more startling. Our life is 'hidden together with Christ in God'. That it is 'hidden' points in part to the fact that Christ is at this time hidden from our view. That does not mean that he is invisible, because he did not ascend to heaven merely in spirit form, but with his resurrected body. So, even though we cannot see him where he now is, he has gone to the place that he is preparing for his people where they will be with him forever (*John* 14:2-4). In that sense it is part of the future hope we are given in the gospel that speaks about the Christian's everlasting home.

There is, however, another sense in which Paul uses this language, one that eloquently expresses the sheer depth of intimacy Christ gives us with God through salvation. It comes out in his High Priestly prayer in John's Gospel in which he prays that his people may be allowed to share in the communion enjoyed within the Godhead through their saving union with him (*John* 17:20-23). It is difficult to find words that adequately express what this means, but Moses captured it with similar eloquence in the Psalms when he said, 'Lord, you have been our dwelling place in all generations' (*Psa.* 90:1).

Even though these Colossian Christians were being distracted by the visible and the tangible in the kind of religion on which they were being fed, and even though we as Christians are so often more taken up with what is seen as opposed to what is unseen, Paul reminds us that we are defined by the invisible reality of where we ultimately belong in Christ.

We are used to defining ourselves by where we belong in earthly terms, 'I am an American', 'I come from Nigeria'. However, it is where we belong in terms of the world to come that defines us ultimately. So much so that Paul is able to tell the Philippians, 'our citizenship is in heaven' (*Phil.* 3:20). That, more than anything, will transform the way we think.

THE PROMISE OF THE FUTURE

The apostle adds one further thought at this point by way of encouragement to act in accordance with his exhortations. 'When Christ who is your life appears, then you also will appear with him in glory' (3:4). The Christ who is invisible to our eyes this present age will one day most certainly come again and when he does, believers who have already died and been taken into glory will appear with him and those who are still on this earth when he comes will immediately be glorified.

It is hard to escape the sheer force of the language Paul employs in this verse. Building on all he has been saying throughout the letter regarding the depth of relationship between Christ and those who believe in him, he reminds the Colossians that Christ 'is your life'. In other words there is no conceiving of a life that is 'Christian' in any kind of isolation from the Christ who alone makes it such. This is something that is profoundly simple and yet so easy to overlook.

What is so significant about this word of encouragement is that it is a 'word' of encouragement. The Colossians were being urged to think that words were not enough when it came to finding fulfillment in the life of faith, that they needed rituals and secret knowledge and mystical experiences to somehow make it authentic.

But Paul's answer throughout has been to point them back to the Word and promise of God in the gospel.

The same has been true for the church and for Christians through the ages. God's Word has been repeatedly portrayed as never being enough and has been supplemented by imagery and architecture, rituals and mystic revelations in order to make it more palatable. But what is missed in all this is the fact that from beginning to end the religion of the Bible has been a word-based religion. What is unique about it is not merely the fact that it purports to be God's Word given through men (which it is), but that God repeatedly links his words to his deeds – his interventions in human history – to allow his words to be put to the test. If his words, whether as promise or prophecy, warning or wisdom, are not proved true through his actions, then they are not worthy of our trust. Of course what transpires as his words unfold over the centuries as the Bible is given is that not one of them has ever failed.

The point of this as far as the Colossians are concerned is that even though some of God's words relate still very much to the future, because the trustworthiness of his words in all that is past has been demonstrated to the full – supremely in relation to Christ – then we have every reason to be sure about them with regard to what is yet to come.

So, as Paul lays down the challenge to set our hearts and minds on Christ and the world which is to come, he is not asking us as Christians to take the biggest gamble of our lives, but instead to build our lives in the present and hope for the future on the greatest reality the world has ever known. It is the reality of the Christ who really came to bring salvation and the Christ who will most certainly come again to call his children home – a hope which stands or falls on the reality of the resurrection (*1 Cor.* 15:14) – and the hope to which Paul rightly points us in this passage. That is what defines the history of our world and universe more than anything else and that is what ought to command our trust and order our lives as we live in its light.

13

The Drastic Side of Holiness

Put to death therefore what is earthly in you: sexual immorality, impurity, passion, evil desire, and covetousness, which is idolatry. ⁶ On account of these the wrath of God is coming. ⁷ In these you too once walked, when you were living in them. ⁸ But now you must put them all away: anger, wrath, malice, slander, and obscene talk from your mouth. ⁹ Do not lie to one another, seeing that you have put off the old self with its practices ¹⁰ and have put on the new self, which is being renewed in knowledge after the image of its creator. ¹¹ Here there is not Greek and Jew, circumcised and uncircumcised, barbarian, Scythian, slave, free; but Christ is all, and in all. (Col. 3:5–11)

There are places in the Gospels where Jesus sounds shocking in the extreme in some of his teachings. One that stands out more than most is where he says in the Sermon on the Mount, 'If your right eye causes you to sin, tear it out and throw it away... and if your right hand causes you to sin, cut it off and throw it away' (*Matt.* 5:29-30). Of course he is not advocating literal self-mutilation, but rather, as he speaks about the seriousness of sin in its effects and consequences, he is calling for drastic action in the way that we deal with it. That is precisely what Paul is advocating as he develops his teaching on what it means for Christians to have died and been raised up together with Christ through their union with him. He is talking about sanctification, that is, what it means to be made holy in God's sight.

Straightaway we are stopped in our tracks and given pause for thought. It is not just that in many Christian circles today the language of holiness has slipped from our vocabulary (ostensibly because it is deemed to be a Puritan or Victorian concept and as such is outdated) but sadly that the very concept of holiness seems to have vanished as well. Many who call themselves Christians embrace lifestyles that are almost indistinguishable from their neighbours who make no such claim about themselves. Apart from the fact that these 'Christians' go to church on at least a semi-regular basis, their values, priorities in life and their moral conduct – at least behind their religious façade – are little different from their non-Christian counterparts. There is nothing that sets them apart from a world that has no time for God.

Yet the idea of being 'set apart from the world' is what lies at the very heart of what the Bible says about holiness. And what the Bible says in that vein is no mere footnote. The Old Testament is full of revelations about God's own holiness and is replete with ethical instruction calling his people to a life of holiness. That strand of teaching is not restricted to the Old Testament. Christ's ministry is full of moral application, as also is the teaching found throughout the New Testament. Indeed, Peter sums it up its full force, quoting from the Old Testament, when he says, 'as he who called you is holy, you also be holy in all your conduct, since it is written, "You shall be holy, for I am holy"' (*1 Pet.* 1:15-16). Holiness mattered then and it still matters now.

As Paul begins to open up his line of reasoning in these verses in relation to what was happening in Colossae it is hard to believe that he is just offering random examples of the kind of sin that is so often present in the church in some generic sense. Rather, as he has become acquainted with this congregation from a distance through his friend Epaphras and through the church's reputation that had already spread far and wide, amidst the good things that were being reported, there were also whispers of certain kinds of conduct and patterns of behaviour that were less than commendable. So it becomes necessary to address those issues in very specific terms in what he has to say here. In so doing he calls these Christians in Colossae to take drastic action in the way they were to deal with the sin that was spoiling their life together in the church.

PUTTING SIN TO DEATH

The very idea of putting anything, let alone anyone, to death is unsettling for many people today. Capital punishment is no longer on the statute books in a growing number of countries and even the need to slaughter animals for food is something that is rarely seen by the average person. But that is the language Paul reaches for in these verses in relation to how we need to deal with sin in our lives as Christians.

It is important to realize that it is indeed to Christians he is speaking in these verses. He is not suggesting that if a person can somehow clean up their life by themselves, by rooting out those things that are offensive to God and to our fellow human beings, that this will somehow commend them to God. Rather, he is saying that only those who already belong to God through the gift of his salvation are able to hear and respond to what God calls for here.

Paul's inclusion of the word 'therefore' (3:5) in this exhortation makes this clear. He is still speaking to those who have died and been raised with Christ through their union with him. But far from being called to a life of genteel respectability, Paul says that the outworking of what that means for them will be seen in their willingness to wage war against sin in all its forms in their life. And this can only be possible because in Christ they have died to their old life which was sinful in its very essence, but have simultaneously been made alive to a whole new life that is characterized by righteousness. More than that, they have been brought into a new kind of life which is empowered and enabled by Christ in a way that is pleasing to God.

The point is this, both for the Colossians as much as for Christians of every age, sin is not something to which we can afford to be indifferent – not merely because it is unacceptable to God, but because it is destructive of all that it means for us to be truly human. Just as a patient dare not ignore the presence of cancer in his or her body, or a gardener ignore the weeds that are quietly taking root in their garden, so neither can a Christian or the church remain indifferent to the destructive power of sin. So serious is it that it cannot be quietly kept under control, it must be rooted out and put to death.

The reason it needs to be dealt with so severely is because it is 'earthly' – or, more literally, 'of the earth' (3:5). Paul has already used that same form of words in the previous passage where he urges his listeners not to set their minds on things that are 'on earth' (3:2). By this he means those things that are part and parcel of the fallenness of this earth, that are part of all that is in rebellion against God. Such things simply have no place in God's new creation and the life of his people.

DEAL WITH SPECIFIC SINS SPECIFICALLY

What follows as the apostle tells his readers what it is they need to 'put to death' (3:5) and 'put away' (3:8) are two lists of particular sins. The first relates to what might be called 'private sins' – either because they are committed away from public view, or else because they are in the hearts and minds of those who commit them.

In the case of 'sexual immorality' (3:5), the many different kinds of behaviour that fall into this category have one thing in common: they are carried out behind closed doors in private. The argument put up by many today in defence of such behaviour is that whatever people do in private is their own business and does not impinge on their public life. But one only has to ask a wife whose husband has been unfaithful, or a female worker with whom the boss has had an affair, only to be abandoned, to realize that it is impossible to draw such neat distinctions. More than that, in biblical terms, what people do in private can never be hidden from God and it has a very real impact on their relationship with him.

When he goes on to speak of 'impurity, passion, evil desire and covetousness, which is idolatry' (3:5), Paul not only speaks of the kind of thoughts and urges that fuel the sexual sins mentioned at the head of this list, but the kinds of impulses that lie behind a whole range of other sins from theft right through to murder.

The very hiddenness of these sins only serves to accentuate the radical action for which Paul calls in order to deal with them. Too often, Christians think that if these sins are simply kept from public view, they can be kept under control. But nothing could be further from the truth. If sin is not dealt with even in its most secret and embryonic form, it will grow into something that is much harder to contain or control and which will do even greater damage to us as individuals and to those around us.

It is not, however, the damage to self or loved ones that Paul cites as the greatest incentive to act on his injunction; it is because 'on account of these things the wrath of God is coming' (3:6). His reference to 'idolatry' (3:5) may well be a kind of summary designation of all the other sins he has identified in that verse, indicating that each in its own way usurps the place of God in our lives and is therefore liable to his judicial wrath.

As if to press this home, Paul reminds the Colossians, 'In these you too once walked when you were living in them' (3:7). This had been their world, their way of life, from which Christ had rescued them. Why, then, were they drifting right back into that old lifestyle? It is a mark of the deceitfulness of sin that it causes spiritual amnesia in those who have been delivered from particular sins. They forget what their conduct did to themselves and others around them.

The second itemized list of sins that Paul outlines has to do with more public sins, in particular, those that affect our relationships with others. He specifically makes mention of, 'anger, wrath, malice, slander and obscene talk' as well as lying to one another (3:8-9). All these in a very real and painful sense are deeply harmful not just to family and community life generally, but to the life of the church as the family of God especially.

The reference to lying is set apart in a sentence of its own for good reason – seen perhaps when it is set over its positive counterpart that Paul mentions in his letter to the Ephesians. There, speaking about the importance of the body life of the church, he says, 'speaking the truth in love, we are to grow up in every way into him who is the head, into Christ' (*Eph.* 4:15). Trust and transparency in communication in all its varied forms are vital to healthy and productive relationships in the life of the church. Yet again he reinforces this exhortation with a reminder to the Colossians that they are not what they once were: 'since you have put off the old self with its sinful practices and have put on the new self' (3:9-10).

The combined force of all that Paul is saying here points to our need as Christians to not only be conscious of the many ways we sin against God and against other people; but, more than that, to be deliberate and ruthless in the way we deal with it. All of this is true because we no longer belong to 'the domain of darkness', but have instead been brought into the kingdom of God's own Son.

That is why Paul adds the qualifying statement, reminding his readers that the 'new self' which they had put on was 'being renewed in knowledge after the image of its creator' (3:10). Once again his choice of words is almost certainly deliberate – picking up on the promise of 'knowledge' of a deeper kind that was being peddled in Colossae. Far from being something these Christians had somehow been deprived of, it lay at the very heart of their experience in the life of faith. Indeed, given the relational as well as informational connotations that the idea of knowledge often carries in Scripture, Paul could hardly have found a richer way to express what they had been given through Christ. The fact that Jesus himself defines the very essence of salvation using this language in his High Priestly prayer says it all. 'And this is eternal life that they know you the only true God and Jesus Christ whom you have sent' (*John* 17:3).

Paul's use of a present continuous tense in what he says points to the transformation that is taking place in the lives of God's people as being a work in progress. But the end product could not be clearer: God's goal in his work of sanctification is to restore us to what he intended us to be as those who bear the image of their Maker.

CHRIST IS ALL IN ALL

Given that this section began with the command to put sin in all its forms to death in our life both individually as Christians and corporately as the church, it may seem more than a little strange to see how Paul rounds off this section. It comes in the form of a bald statement: 'Here there is not Greek and Jew, circumcised and uncircumcised, barbarian, Scythian, slave, free, but Christ is all and in all' (3:11). How does this tie in with all that has come before? The answer has to be that he has in mind the way salvation is seen to be worked out in the life of the church.

The 'here' to which he points in this verse can only make sense as a reference to the church – or more specifically, the church in its local expression in the congregation in Colossae. If the sins that Paul had identified in the preceding verses were the root cause of the damage that was being done to its fellowship, then the ultimate reason why those sins needed to be dealt with was Christ and all that his redemption had secured.

The theme the apostle picks up on at this point is one that he mentions overtly and using similar language in two other places in his letters (*1 Cor.* 12:13; *Gal.* 3:28). The note he is sounding is the fact that the redemption found in Christ is no respecter of race, class, culture, gender or any other qualifier that might cause us to segregate our fellow members of the human race. The reason he both chooses and needs to repeat this theme is because the tendency to do just that is so ingrained in our fallen human psyche. And, evidently, as Paul addresses the various sins that needed to be dealt with specifically in the Colossian church, a significant symptom of the damage they were causing could be seen at this level. People in the church were being treated according to their outward classification as opposed to what they had become in Christ.

One distinctive of the point Paul is making here in this verse over against the similar-sounding references in Corinthians and Galatians, is the scope of what he says about Christ: 'but Christ is all and in all'. We noted back in the first chapter of this letter Paul's monumental statement about Christ that 'in him all things hold together' (1:17). In other words, the apostle wants to impress on his readers that there is a cosmic dimension to Christ's saving work that goes beyond the mere salvation of people. But, that said, the scope of his saving work is able to reach into every nook and cranny of our diverse race, bringing people from every conceivable background into the fellowship of his family. In that sense, Christ is not only the key to dealing with sin in our lives personally; but also the key to enable us to deal with the sin that divides our shared life corporately within the church.

Even though Paul's call to Christians to deal with sin by 'putting it to death' may sound drastic to our ears, it is nothing compared to the drastic measures that were required on Christ's part to deal with it once for all by taking the sins of his people on himself and suffering the penalty which those sins deserve through his own death on the cross. That puts our responsibility as Christians in its true perspective.

14

Cultivating a Life of Holiness – Together

Put on then, as God's chosen ones, holy and beloved, compassion,
kindness, humility, meekness, and patience, [13] *bearing with one an-*
other and, if one has a complaint against another, forgiving each
other; as the Lord has forgiven you, so you also must forgive. [14] *And*
above all these put on love, which binds everything together in perfect
harmony. [15] *And let the peace of Christ rule in your hearts, to which*
indeed you were called in one body. And be thankful. [16] *Let the word*
of Christ dwell in you richly, teaching and admonishing one another
in all wisdom, singing psalms and hymns and spiritual songs, with
thankfulness in your hearts to God. [17] *And whatever you do, in word*
or deed, do everything in the name of the Lord Jesus, giving thanks to
God the Father through him. (Col. 3:12–17)

For many people holiness is often perceived in negative terms. It conjures up images of an austere life where joy and pleasure do not belong. For such people the language Paul uses about holiness in the previous section resonates with them, because to them it is all about putting sin to death and putting off anything that might lead us to sin. However, even though what an older generation called 'mortification of sin' is indeed an essential part in growing in holiness; it is by no means all that it involves. As we read on into what Paul says next in this passage, it very quickly becomes apparent that what that older generation of Christians called 'vivification' is even more important. If the gardener we mentioned in the last chapter was only concerned with uprooting weeds and cutting away undergrowth, the 'garden' he ended up with would be little more than bare earth. His whole goal is to cultivate a place of beauty and pleasure. So too, then, as Christ, the Master Gardener, does his work in the lives of his people, his concern is to transform them, not just personally but together as his family, into something that is truly 'set apart' as beautifully different from this dilapidated world.

This stands out in Paul's choice of words in these verses. Over against the 'put to death' and 'put away' language he has just been using he now talks about what we as Christians must 'put on' (3:12, 14) instead. More than that, this whole exercise is one that we pursue together as God's new community and not just by ourselves. Once again this becomes clear when we recognize the contrast between this passage and the one that came before. There the apostle was pointing out the kind of sins that disrupt and divide the fellowship of the church; but here he highlights those attitudes of heart and mind and the kind of behaviour that will instead build relationships, cultivating peace and harmony in the household of believers.

Once more Paul gently reminds his readers that all of this can be true only because, as Christians, they have been 'raised with Christ' (3:1). In the previous paragraph he flagged up that connection with the word 'therefore' (3:5). In this paragraph he notes it with the word 'then' (3:12). No aspect of our pursuit of holiness is an isolated private enterprise. From beginning to end it can only truly happen as it grows out of our new life in fellowship with Jesus Christ – the One in whom we are 'God's chosen ones, holy and beloved' (3:12).

As the Colossians had been taken in by the teaching of those who had been influencing their church, their eyes had been taken off Christ and in so doing they had lost sight of who they really were as his people. Paul is at pains to remind them of the whole new identity they had been given in Christ and, in light of that, to call them to live accordingly. What was true for the Colossians in their own unique set of circumstances remains true for all Christians everywhere. We need to understand what we have become through faith in Christ and then live in light of who we are in fellowship with him.

THE INGREDIENTS OF HOLY LIVING

We have already noted in a number of ways the corporate character of the holiness Paul has in view here. We have also seen how Paul has made reference to what it means for us as human beings to be made in the image and likeness of God. What we have not done, however, is to see how closely those two thoughts are related.

All too often when we think about the image of God in man, and what it means for us as human beings to be made in his 'likeness' (*Gen.* 1:26) we conceive of it in individualistic terms. Even though there is a very real personal dimension to it, there is something far greater in view: namely the way that we as a race were made to reflect God's glory and majesty together.

The God in whose image we have been made is the God who is the holy Trinity. Although he is one God, he is at the same time one God in three Persons: Father, Son and Holy Spirit. His entire existence is one of unity within diversity and diversity expressed in unity that serves only to magnify his glory. So, just as he exists in eternal relationship, it then follows that those who bear his likeness in his creation do so also in relationship. And just as sin has disrupted and destroyed our relationships on the human level as much as with God, then so too salvation must restore those relationships on both levels.

As we look, then, at what Paul calls these Christians in Colossae to 'put on' as they grow in the faith and grow in holiness, all the attitudes and types of behaviour he identifies have to do with renewing relationships with our fellow human beings – beginning with those in the church. There is a place for delving into what each of them means in detail, but what they all have in common is the fact they all express a concern for others that is greater than our concern for self.

If sin, as Martin Luther famously said, leaves us 'turned in upon ourselves', then the very essence of salvation as God's antidote to sin must reverse that distortion of our heart. Not only does it turn us out from ourselves and point us upwards towards God, it also turns us outward towards our fellow men. As Paul puts it in his letter to the Philippians, 'Let each of you look not only to his own interests, but to the interests of others' (*Phil.* 2:4). The false teachers in Colossae were able to gain a foothold in the hearts of their hearers because they preyed on that spirit of self-interest that is so deeply rooted in the human heart and which lingers on, even after a person comes to faith in Christ. Paul's concern is to show them that their new relationship with Christ is inseparable from the new relationship into which they have been brought with their fellow-Christians.

Wonderful and all as that sounds on paper, the apostle knows only too well how relationships in church can often feel just as blighted, if not more so, as those in the world. The difference, however, is that as Christians we have a whole new framework within which we can deal with those damaged relationships and Paul goes on to spell that out here. After listing the kind of qualities of attitude and conduct these Christians ought to cultivate, he says, 'and if one has a complaint against another, forgiving one another; as the Lord has forgiven you, so you also must forgive' (3:13).

That relatively simple statement carries monumental significance which reverberates through the teaching of Christ through into the apostolic teaching of the New Testament. We see it in the way Jesus punctuates his teaching of the Lord's Prayer in the Sermon on the Mount (*Matt.* 6:14-15). We hear it too in what Paul says to the Ephesians about guarding relationships in God's family (*Eph.* 4:32). So here he reminds the Colossians that they do not have the luxury of living with one set of rules under which God relates to them (through forgiveness) and a different set of rules through which they relate to others (in which forgiveness is optional). No, if they have indeed received forgiveness from God through the Lord Jesus Christ, then they too 'must forgive' (3:13). Forgiveness and a forgiving spirit on both levels are essential ingredients to holiness of life.

THE HEART OF A HOLY LIFE

Paul draws together the individual threads of attitude and action listed in the previous verses in what he says in the next two. He speaks about the importance of peace and love as the hallmarks of God's family, but introduces what he says with the words 'And above all these things put on love, which binds everything together in perfect harmony' (3:14). Important as each individual ingredient of corporate holiness may be, as outlined above, they are nothing in themselves unless they are wrapped up in something greater and that something is love.

It would be very easy to lose sight of the significance of that statement in today's world when we think of a similar-sounding statement in the famous Lennon and McCartney song: 'All you need is Love!' Were they just saying the same thing as Paul, but just two thousand years later? The answer, of course, is 'No!' The Beatles' idea of love and that which we find in the Bible are very different.

The human heart is no stranger to the concept of love or to the deep-seated yearning to find it; but likewise it knows only too well that it can mean different things in different contexts. In the Greek and Roman world in which the Colossians were living, it had been neatly categorized into different types of 'love' in different kinds of relationship from friendship, to family to its most intimate expression between a man and a woman. In our world it has almost universally been reduced to a sentimental feeling that has more to do with hormones and personal chemistry than any kind of meaningful bond.

Paul does not leave his readers to guess what he has in mind as he uses the language of love here. The kind of love with which Christians ought literally to 'clothe' themselves is the same kind of love with which God himself is clothed and which he has so freely lavished upon them as his 'beloved' (3:12). In both references he uses the Greek word for love that had effectively been commandeered by the church to capture the uniqueness of the love that is not only found in God, but which he also pours out on his people in salvation. When it is viewed in its broad sweep as that divine love revealed in Scripture, what makes it stands out is the fact that it is the love of self-sacrificing commitment. In particular, it is the love God expresses through the covenant he enters with his people – a relationship which has been well described as 'the bond of love'. A bond that was ratified ultimately through the blood of Jesus shed upon the cross.

For the Colossians to be reminded of the kind of love that undergirded their very existence as a church would have come as a sobering challenge to the divisive influences that were gaining momentum in their midst through the false teaching they were hearing. In their scale of priorities they could not afford to lose sight of the thing that matters most.

The fact that this kind of love 'binds everything together in perfect harmony' is not just a plain statement of how God's love impacts people's lives, but is actually also an echo of something Paul said at an earlier point in his letter. Over against the kind of ideas that were being taught in Colossae about how things hold together in the universe, Paul had said regarding Christ, 'in him all things hold together' (1:17) – he is the secret to the harmony of the universe. So here, in a more pointed and practical way, the apostle is saying that we enter more fully into that peace and harmony through salvation.

For that reason he then goes on to say, by way of direct exhortation, 'And let the peace of Christ rule in your hearts, to which indeed you were called in one body' (1:15). Christ's blood-bought peace is to rule in the hearts of his people. It is not to be there as some kind of warm and fuzzy feeling; but as the key controlling factor that actually governs the way they relate to one another.

It is more than striking to see the frequency with which this theme surfaces in Scripture and the weight that is attached to it when it does. Jesus makes it a key concern in his prayer for the church on the eve of his crucifixion (*John* 17:20-26) – referring not only to the quality of oneness that salvation brings into God's family, but making it clear that preserving that oneness affects the credibility of the gospel. Paul uses equally forceful language in what he says to the Ephesians as he expounds the impact the gospel has on our life in community. As he begins to apply the truths and principles he has been expounding he says, 'Spare no effort to preserve the unity of the Spirit in the bond of peace' (*Eph.* 4:3) – my translation.

It is perhaps curious to note that although the apostle sets out holiness and oneness as being integrally related, too often that connection has not been made in the minds of Christians and not infrequently among those who have been most vocal about the importance of holiness. Yet, if we really grasp the kind of life to which we have been called in the gospel – collectively as much as individually – then we will appreciate how vital it is, not just for our enjoyment of life in God's family, but also for our witness to the world.

THE MEANS TO CULTIVATING HOLINESS

Given the weight of the challenge bound up with this lengthy exhortation about holiness that Paul has been issuing in this chapter, it is not hard to see how the Colossians may have been feeling more than a little daunted over how they could begin to work it out in practice. Even the frequent reminders that had pointed them back to Christ needed to be fleshed out more pointedly if they were to make something of them in their lives and relationships. But that is precisely what Paul does as he draws the threads of this section together. He identifies two things in particular that are the primary means by which Christians are enabled to grow in holiness in their lives personally as well as in the life of the church corporately.

The first is 'the word of Christ' (3:16). By this he did not mean the 'words' (plural) of Christ as a special category of God's revelation. Christians have often been mistakenly led to think in those terms through 'red-letter' versions of the Bible, but fail to realize that his words are no different from God's words as they are found in all of Scripture (*2 Tim.* 3:16). Rather, he has in mind the message of Jesus as the Christ which is the heart and substance of all that God has revealed in Scripture. Appreciating the Christ-centredness of the Bible was and still is the primary means God uses to make his people holy.

At one level there is nothing new in that. Paul's audience would have been familiar enough with the Old Testament teachings to realize from passages like Psalm 119 that God uses his Word to re-order and reshape the lives of his people in salvation. They may even have been aware of Paul's own teaching that linked transformation of life with the power of God's Word (*Rom.* 6:17; 12:1-2). And it is not beyond the bounds of possibility that they may even have heard references to Christ's high priestly prayer in which he said explicitly, 'Sanctify them in the truth; your word is truth' (*John* 17:17). But what comes out here is the way Paul applies that truth to them in particular. The Word of Christ is to 'dwell in [them] richly'. That is, Christ as the heart of God's message in his Word was to permeate and saturate them in every way. So much so that it will shape the way they minister to one another in the church 'teaching and admonishing one another in all wisdom'.

However, Paul goes further as he spells out the extent to which the message of Christ ought to impact their lives. It should spill over into their singing 'psalms and hymns and spiritual songs in [their] hearts to God' (3:16). What is so interesting about the way Paul's thought unfolds in this verse is the fact that 'the word of

Christ' of which he speaks should not only permeate the teaching of the church, but also its worship through song. Indeed, the fact that he includes both in the same sentence shows how the sung praise of the church is to be instructive and edifying in a way that reinforces the different expressions of its teaching ministry. By making this connection the apostle is simply bearing out the fact that the use of 'psalms, hymns and spiritual songs' is one of the greatest didactic tools the church has. This has been proved true in the durability of the great hymns of the church through the centuries and should continue to prove true in the kind of compositions that each generation adds to the repertoire of songs compiled for the worship of God.

CHRIST: THE KEY TO HOLINESS

Paul has been pretty far-reaching in what he has said in this wider section about holiness and how it is to be pursued by God's people and in the next section he will move on to specific sets of relationships and how they too come within its orbit. But before he launches into those specifics, he pauses and says, 'And whatever you do, in word or deed, do everything in the name of the Lord Jesus, giving thanks to God the Father through him' (3:17).

The reference to 'word and deed' is a summary reminder of what he has been saying in this extended passage: namely, that just as sin has tainted everything in our life without Christ, so holiness likewise must touch everything as we live out our new life in fellowship with him. But why does he tell these Christians in Colossae that they are to 'do everything in the name of the Lord Jesus'? Clearly Paul was not suggesting they should invoke the name of Jesus as some kind of Christian mantra; but, rather, to live out their new life with a conscious awareness of its being 'in him' in every conceivable sense. The spiritual mentors who had crept in among them were offering a form of Christianity in which, at best, Christ was being marginalized; but Paul tirelessly calls these Christians back to him.

That perhaps explains why not once, but three times in three consecutive verses Paul has urged these people to act with thankfulness in their heart. Since they had been seduced into thinking they needed something extra to fulfil the calling God had given them and since Paul throughout this letter has been reminding them in every conceivable way that this was not the case, because they had Christ and he was all they needed; so they should be filled with thankfulness for all that he means to them as his people. Even though in one sense Paul is being case-specific to the needs of the Colossian Church, he is at the same time sounding a note that needs to be heard by Christians and churches throughout the ages. We can never be thankful enough to God for all he has done for us and given to us through his Son!

15

Relating to Others
as We Relate to the Lord

Wives, submit to your husbands, as is fitting in the Lord. [19] *Husbands, love your wives, and do not be harsh with them.* [20] *Children, obey your parents in everything, for this pleases the Lord.* [21] *Fathers, do not provoke your children, lest they become discouraged.* [22] *Slaves, obey in everything those who are your earthly masters, not by way of eye-service, as people-pleasers, but with sincerity of heart, fearing the Lord.* [23] *Whatever you do, work heartily, as for the Lord and not for men,* [24] *knowing that from the Lord you will receive the inheritance as your reward. You are serving the Lord Christ.* [25] *For the wrongdoer will be paid back for the wrong he has done, and there is no partiality.* [1] *Masters, treat your slaves justly and fairly, knowing that you also have a Master in heaven.* (Col. 3:18–4:1)

The 'everything' that dominated the last verse of the previous section and which may have sounded somewhat vague and general suddenly becomes very specific. Paul now takes the profound principles bound up with what it means for Christians to have died and been raised to life through their relationship with Christ and begins to apply them to a range of relationships that are meant to represent every kind of relationship we may have. He wants his readers to realize that our relationship with Christ must inevitably colour and control our relationship with everyone.

What is so striking about what he says in this passage is not so much the challenge it presents to us as Christians as we begin to discover the cost of being Christlike in our relationships, but that such relationships are so very different from the norm in a Christless world. This would of course have said a lot to the Christians in Colossae as they reflected on what Paul had been saying about holiness as the great distinctive of the Christian life over against

[109]

what their newfound teachers had been saying. There is nothing mystical and esoteric about holiness of life, it is deeply practical and down to earth in the difference it makes to life in its totality.

The practicality of what Paul covers in this section – especially as it touches upon everyday relationships and everyday life – is echoed in many parts of the Bible in a way that brings home the earthiness of the Christian religion. It is not a faith that needs to get dressed up in special clothes to go on display before a watching world; its clothing (as we saw from the language of 'putting off' and 'putting on' earlier in this chapter) is that of changed lives and renewed relationships. The significance of that could not be more far-reaching with regard to the way it advertises the gospel. Paul sums it up in a similar passage in his letter to Titus when, speaking to slaves about how they relate to their masters, he says that as they do so in a Christlike manner, 'in everything they may adorn the doctrine of God our Saviour' (*Titus* 2:10). Transformed lives and relationships in every sphere of life become the most powerful proof that God's promise of salvation in the gospel is real.

The new 'gospel' that was gaining traction in Colossae – whatever its precise details may have been – was more concerned with finding an escape from the harsh realities of life through secret knowledge and mystical rites and experience than providing rescue. In that sense, it is not unlike many other expressions of a so-called Christian faith that are more about spiritual escapism than redemption and renewal. The gospel of Christ Jesus as Lord that lies at the very heart of everything Paul says in this letter could not be more different. As we begin to look in detail at the impact it has on people's lives and relationships, we start to see why.

MARRIAGE TO THE GLORY OF GOD

The opening line in this section of practical application is one that cannot but jar with many modern readers: 'Wives, submit to your husbands' (3:18) – it is so jarring that most people don't manage to read on to the end of the sentence. The idea of submission is increasingly unpopular in contemporary culture, at least in the Western world. However, it would be naïve to think that the same kind of resistance to the idea of submission has not been present in every culture through all of history.

There is something deep within the human spirit that cherishes the notion of personal autonomy, and even though it has very often been repressed in one way or another, it never quite goes away. The Bible explains where that spirit comes from at the very beginning of Genesis when it talks about man's fall and how sin came into the world. When the serpent suggested to Eve that if she ate the forbidden fruit she and her husband would 'be like God' (*Gen.* 3:5), it was alluring in the extreme. It seemed to spell perfect freedom and independence. And so from that point onwards in the history of our race, human beings have yearned for individual autonomy insofar as they can afford and grasp it.

Despite the apparent bluntness of what the apostle says here, he is saying much more than what many people see through a mere cursory glance at the text. Far from advocating a view of marriage which is repressive for women, he is actually offering a glimpse of something that alters the whole dynamic of that relationship. Far from its becoming an arena for competing control, it becomes a reflection of the most extraordinary relationship in the universe.

The key to understanding what Paul is saying here is the qualifier he adds to his exhortation: 'as is fitting in the Lord'. By this he is not merely saying that such submission on the part of wives to their husbands is what is expected in Christian marriages as some kind of arbitrary code; but that the relationship of Christian marriage is radically transformed through relationship with Christ – even where only one spouse is a Christian. The fact that a wife is 'in the Lord' – that expression and thought that has been cropping up again and again in Colossians – means that her relationship with Christ makes the world of a difference to her relationship with her husband.

How is that so? Because the way that Jesus as the Son of God in human flesh relates to his heavenly Father becomes the template for all relationships in which his children find themselves. We have already noted that, as human beings, we have been made in the image and likeness of God. That image was deeply damaged through man's sin and rebellion, but the whole purpose of God in redemption is to rescue and restore his family likeness in the lives of all who come to faith in his son, our Saviour Jesus Christ. And, again as we have been seeing, such is the extent of that redemption in Christ that it not only transforms the way we relate to God, but also the way we relate to others.

What is so striking about this is that the inclusion of 'in the Lord' makes the Christian wives and women who read this passage look away from what they are in themselves to what they have become in Christ. And in particular to look at the way that Jesus' coming to be our Saviour involved a submission of monumental proportions, but he was not forced into it; instead he willingly and voluntarily put himself at his Father's disposal knowing that it was for the glory of God and the ultimate good of his people.

Even though there is no explicit repetition of that 'in the Lord' phrase in what Paul says to husbands, there is every reason to see its being implicitly carried over. The idea of a Christian's being 'in the Lord' is so deeply embedded in all that he says not only in this letter, but all his letters, that for Paul it is simply impossible for a person to think of themselves as a Christian without thinking of their union with Christ.

So the positive injunction to husbands, 'love your wives' and its negative counterpart, 'do not be harsh with them' (3:19) is not some arbitrary expectation for those who 'join the club' of the Christian community; but, rather, it is an extension of what they themselves have become in Christ. Just as he has loved them and not been harsh in his dealings with these men, so his love and gentleness flow over into the way they treat their wives.

The stresses and strains of married life were as much a part of life in Colossae as they are today in a world where the very institution of marriage is in crisis because of rising divorce rates on the one hand and growing disillusionment with marriage on the other. In one sense it is gratifying to see the number of books on marriage that are appearing to try and reverse those trends, especially from Christian authors; but all too often they have one inherent flaw. They end up being little more than another 'how to' manual that spell out codes of conduct for husbands and wives to follow. And even where their focus is the need to cultivate an 'authentic' relationship between husband and wife, all too often the key ingredient to genuine authenticity is missing: namely that vital relationship with God through Jesus Christ that not only provides the pattern for all our relationships, but the power to live them out.

THE FAMILY WITHIN GOD'S FAMILY

It is quite natural that Paul should shift his attention from the relationship of husbands and wives in marriage to that of parents and children in families. Here again he relates the relationships of life in human families to that supreme relationship that we find in God's family that defines and controls all others. This time the expression Paul uses is, 'for this pleases the Lord' (3:20). Here again, even though he attaches this qualifier to what he says to children, there is every reason to believe that he implies it just as much in what he says to fathers, for all the reasons stated above.

It is important to bear in mind that the apparent neatness of what Paul is describing here in terms of what has so often been called the 'nuclear family' should not obscure the range of relevance in what he is saying to every other expression of family life. Even though the number of 'different' families has increased exponentially around the world in recent history, those expressions of family life where there has been separation, divorce, bereavement, or no marriage in the first place, have all been around since the beginning of time. What is so striking and yet is so often overlooked is the fact that when Jesus was on this earth he did not avoid those 'families'. The whole purpose in his coming was not only to rescue and redeem individuals in isolation, but the web of relationships in which they are found. It is of the very essence of what God spells out in his covenant of grace in salvation that he is concerned about our relationships in life as much as what we are as individuals.

So, as we look at the specifics of what Paul says here to those within the web of family relationships we see how a person's relationship with Christ leaves its mark on every other relationship to which they belong.

To children (of believing parents) he says, 'obey your parents in everything, for this pleases the Lord' (3:20). It would be a mistake to think that Paul is merely setting out a bare obligation that he lays on children in this command and adding 'for this pleases the Lord' as a kind of sweetener. Even though that is true in an isolated sense, it does not fit with the wider flow of what Paul has been saying in this letter. The only reason the apostle has confidence in telling anyone – children included – what God expects of them and then

[113]

expect them to be able and willing to comply is because of all he has said about God's saving and transforming grace in Christ. And as he addresses the children of Christian homes directly at this point – regardless of their age or stage of development – he does so with the confidence that the Christ who gave their parent or parents ears to hear and hearts to respond to his Word, is well able to do the same for their offspring.

Likewise in addressing fathers who in Paul's world of the first century A.D. were just as prone to exasperating their children as are fathers in the twenty-first century, he is able to challenge what is a natural tendency in human beings only because he believes in the supernatural power of the gospel to change those tendencies. The protocols of family life in the Roman world were such that a father would not expect to be challenged in this way – 'my house, my rules' meant much more then than it does today – but it was Christian fathers in that Roman world that Paul was addressing.

Families are the cradle of society and civilization in more ways than one, yet it is in our families that we see the earliest display of the breakdown of both. As Paul speaks into what so often has been the hopelessness of family life gone wrong, he is able to hold out hope – because of Christ.

FREED UP TO BE THE PERFECT SLAVE

As Paul now turns his attention to another set of relationships, that of slaves to their masters, all kinds of questions pop up before we can even begin to consider the detail of what he says. (And, interestingly, he goes into much greater detail in this sphere of relationships than he does with those of marriage and family life.)

At one level there is the question as to why the Bible and perhaps the New Testament especially is all but silent on the institution of slavery which was and still is an affront to human rights and dignity. Does the fact that Paul and other biblical writers simply accept it without question mean that they secretly condone the practice of slavery? The answer to that has to be 'No', not just because Paul does actually begin to challenge it, however surreptitiously, in Philemon, but more so because the apostolic mission was not primarily to Christianize the world, but to proclaim the gospel of salvation.

At another level the question arises as to why, out of all the other sets of relationships that Paul could have referred to at this point, does he opt for this one? (It is a question that is bolstered by the fact that he follows the same pattern in Ephesians and Titus.) Without being definitive, it is likely that he deliberately reaches for this example at the extreme end of the spectrum of relationships on the premise that if God's grace in salvation can transform relationships in that sphere, it can do so in every other sphere of relationships in between.

What, then, does Paul say to slaves and their masters? Following on from what we have noted already, we cannot help but be struck by his even more frequent references in these verses to the relationship these [Christian] slaves and masters have with Christ as being the determining factor in the way they relate to each other. They are to do so 'fearing the Lord' (3:22), 'as for the Lord' (3:23), 'serving the Lord' (3:24) and 'knowing that you have a Master in heaven' (4:1). The apostle simply will not allow his Christian readers to forget the fact that they now are what they are 'in Christ' and everything about how they relate to others is shaped and moulded by how Christ relates to them and them to him. The relentlessness of his repetition of this point highlights the stubbornness, even of the Christian heart, to grasp this new reality.

What stands out in Paul's injunction to slaves in light of the all-controlling principle of their being in fellowship with Christ is the fact that he can call them to the kind of submission and devotion to their masters that is genuine. 'Slaves, obey in everything those who are your earthly masters, not by way of eye-service, as people-pleasers, but with sincerity of heart' (3:22). More than that, he can encourage them to 'work heartily' (3:23). Nothing could have been more counter-cultural to the world of slavery in Paul's day and nothing could be further from what is so often the norm within the hierarchies of the workplace in ours. He was calling for the type of behaviour that was radically different from what this world expects.

The reason he can appeal to Christian slaves in this way and expect them to comply with his exhortations is because they, along with him, no longer live with this world as their dominant horizon in life. Hence his saying to them, 'knowing that from the

Lord you will receive the inheritance as your reward' (3:24) – 'the inheritance' being the new heaven and the new earth promised to all who trust in Christ. Paul also points to the darker side of that horizon when he warns, 'For the wrongdoer will be paid back for the wrong he has done, and there is no partiality' (3:25). The future life holds not only the promise of everlasting blessing for those who live by faith, but the threat of never-ending consequences for those who do not.

That thought of the future is still in Paul's mind in the one-line exhortation he gives to those who are slave masters. 'Masters, treat your slaves justly and fairly, knowing that you also have a Master in heaven' (4:1). Even though Christian slave-owners as much as any other slave-owner of that time would have instinctively leaned towards the norms of conduct of their time in the way they treated their slaves, as the apostle pointed them to Christ he reminded them that their relationship with him brought a whole new perspective into their life.

It is that new horizon that Christians have in Christ, by virtue of their lives being bound up in his life, that the future takes on a whole new significance in such a way that every aspect of their present life is transformed. Our relationship with him alters how we relate to everyone else.

16

Praying and Living for What Matters Most

Continue steadfastly in prayer, being watchful in it with thanksgiv-
ing. *³At the same time, pray also for us, that God may open to us*
a door for the word, to declare the mystery of Christ, on account of
which I am in prison – *⁴that I may make it clear, which is how I*
ought to speak. *⁵Conduct yourselves wisely toward outsiders, mak-*
ing the best use of the time. *⁶Let your speech always be gracious,*
seasoned with salt, so that you may know how you ought to answer
each person. (Col. 4:2–6)

Much of what Paul has been saying throughout this letter
has been geared towards challenging the priorities of the
Christians in Colossae. The influence of the false teachers in their
church has had the effect of deflecting the focus of their faith away
from Christ to lesser things and, in so doing, shifted the focus of
their life away from the things that matter most in God's kingdom,
to things which matter little by comparison. The apostle sounds
that same note here as he transitions into the closing section of
what he has to say.

Having spent the last chapter and more issuing exhortations to
his readers that arise directly out of all he has expounded in relation to the centrality of Christ to the gospel, he continues in that
same vein, but this time in more general terms. He moves from
applying what he has been saying about union with Christ in the
personal life of believers and the internal life of God's family to
the impact of the gospel on the unbelieving world in which they
find themselves.

That shift is in itself significant because what had been happening in the church in Colossae was not dissimilar to what happens in
many churches when distracting influences surface in their midst.

Almost invariably they become so caught up with the internal affairs and problems of the church that they lose sight of their calling to be salt and light in the world (*Matt.* 5:13-16). Paul's closing exhortations are designed to point them back to that calling as they live out their new life in fellowship with Christ before the watching world.

Paul's concerns crystallize in a number of important ways. In the first place they are far bigger than just what is going on in Colossae. Even though the believers there were absorbed by the challenges of their own local situation, the apostle reminds them of the wider Christian world to which they belonged and of which he was very much a part. So he gently reminds them of his own work and his need of prayer in all he was doing.

Flowing out of that, in the second place, is Paul's passionate desire to get the gospel out to a world that is in spiritual darkness. He points to this not just in relation to his own particular calling to proclaim the gospel of Christ, but also to the Colossians themselves and their calling to bear witness to Christ in their own community.

The third issue that binds the other two together is the importance of prayer in every aspect of the Christian life – something that, as with many Christians and churches, was simply going by default in the midst of all that was going on in Colossae.

These concerns are no mere random loose ends that Paul bundles into the closing remarks at the end of his letter, but rather a careful restatement of things that are of the utmost importance to the church of all ages as God's people live out their calling in the world. Paul's reminders to these people in Asia Minor deserve repetition to the church in our own time.

CULTIVATE THE DISCIPLINE OF PRAYER

The fact that Paul finds it necessary to say, 'continue steadfastly in prayer' (4:2) suggests that the discipline of prayer had lapsed somewhat in the church in Colossae. What had begun as a vital component of church life after Epaphras planted the church in their city had by now at best begun to falter and at worst may have almost lapsed completely. Indeed the fact that a few verses later Paul points to their founding minister and says he is 'always struggling on your behalf in his prayers' (4:12) would suggest that he was more concerned about the spiritual condition and welfare of the Colossian Christians than they were themselves. Indeed, given that the word translated 'struggling' might be more literally rendered 'agonizing', we gather something of the sense of urgency in this man's praying.

One of the most striking features of the extraordinary expansion of the early church, recorded as it is in the opening chapters of the book of Acts, is the link between gospel growth and fervent prayer on the part of those early believers. Right from the outset after the 3,000 people came to faith under Peter's preaching on the Day of Pentecost we are told that of the four things to which they 'devoted themselves' prayer was one of them (*Acts* 2:42). More than that, the regularity and the intensity of their times of prayer are almost invariably linked by Luke to the way the gospel continued to spread with remarkable speed in the chapters that follow.

The new ideas about spirituality that had been introduced in Colossae had succeeded in relegating prayer to the edges of church life and, if the main thrust of Epaphras' prayer was anything to go by, that these Christians might 'stand mature and fully assured in the will of God' (4:12), it would appear that they were wavering in their faith and usefulness as a consequence. Prayer has had and must always have a vital place in the life of the church as much as in the lives of Christians individually if we are to grow spiritually and be effective with the gospel in our witness to the world. Hence the need to persevere in it, overcoming the lethargy and distractions that so often stifle it.

As often is the case when Paul gives instruction about prayer, he does not merely encourage his readers to pray; but to do so 'being watchful in it and with thanksgiving' (4:2). The reference to watchfulness echoes what Jesus said to his own disciples in the Garden of Gethsemane to 'watch and pray that you may not enter into temptation' (*Mark* 14:38). It carries the sense of being alert and aware of the circumstances in which we live. That would have had a real resonance with the Colossian Christians who had allowed themselves to be lulled into a measure of spiritual torpor regarding the influences that were changing the course of their church.

The 'thanksgiving' that was also to play a part in their praying was no perfunctory acknowledgement of God's answers to prayer in the past. The fact, as we saw earlier, that Paul deliberately emphasizes the place of thankfulness, particularly for salvation in all its component parts, in the Christian life (3:15-17), helps us to appreciate why he echoes it again at this point. In its deepest sense prayer is a very tangible expression of our communion with God through Christ in which every answer he gives to our prayers becomes a catalyst for our ever-deepening appreciation of God and his grace.

REMEMBER THOSE WHO PROCLAIM THE GOSPEL

As Paul specifically encourages the church in Colossae to faithfully cultivate their life of prayer, he becomes even more specific when he asks them to remember him and his own ministry in particular. It was not unusual for the apostle to ask for prayer in this way, but it is telling that he does so with such frequency.

Despite his very obvious personal qualities and abilities and despite the high esteem in which he was held in the eyes of many in the New Testament world, he never saw it as beneath his dignity or beyond his need to solicit the prayers of others. So, here, he urges the Colossians, 'At the same time pray also for us' (4:3). Even though Paul was so often perceived as the helper to these churches, he was always deeply conscious of his own need of help to pursue his calling and remain faithful to his Lord. Indeed, speaking to the Christians in Corinth – who were so much in need of his help in many ways – he unashamedly says, 'You also must help us by prayer' (*2 Cor.* 1:11). No preacher of the gospel or leader in the church is beyond needing the help of all God's people as they pray.

Paul's particular concern as he asked the Colossians to pray for him was in relation to his ability to spread the gospel. At one level there was a very real practical restriction on him in this regard because he was writing from prison (4:3). The question of which of his imprisonments he had in mind is discussed in the Introduction to this commentary, but as was indicated there, it is more than likely that it was the house arrest under which he was placed in Rome and which is recorded for us at the end of Acts.

His desire was that 'God may open a door for the word, to declare the mystery of Christ… that I may make it clear, which is how I ought to speak' (4:3, 4). Given the fact that his freedom was seriously curtailed, there was a very real limit imposed on how far he could go with his message in the literal sense of being able to move around freely. So he is certainly asking that God would give opportunities for him to proclaim the message of Christ; but at the same time, by asking for the right words in his presentation of that message, he was very much aware of his need of divine help to make it effective in the hearts of his hearers.

Too often preachers and their preaching can be taken for granted. (Indeed, too often preachers take themselves and their own gifts for granted as well!) But Paul gives a healthy reminder to us that if we are to see the success of any gospel ministry, it needs the support of the prayers of God's people.

LIVE AND SPEAK TO POINT THE WORLD TO JESUS

Paul moves from encouraging a disciplined approach to prayer generally in the life of the church, and urging prayer specifically for the success of the gospel to calling on these Christians to live and speak in a way that will make an impact on the unbelieving world around them.

He exhorts them to 'conduct [themselves] wisely towards outsiders, making the best use of the time' (4:5). The fact Paul has to remind his readers of their duty to 'outsiders' is not without significance. It would appear, as we suggested a few moments ago, that these Christians in Colossae had become so preoccupied with what was going on in the church that they had simply forgotten that the drama of their life was being played out before an audience of 'outsiders' in the watching world. That Paul needed to caution them to live 'wisely' before those who were watching would suggest that their conduct and conversation had become something less than that.

Too often it is the case that Christians become so self-absorbed and inward-looking that they are simply oblivious to how they are perceived by their unbelieving neighbours. More than that, it does not seem to cross their mind that the way they are perceived by those who are not yet Christians has a profound effect on how the gospel is perceived.

When Paul qualifies his exhortation about how the Colossians are to live with the words '... making the best use of the time'

[121]

(4:5), it would appear that he saying much more than just, 'Don't waste it!' The fact the he speaks not merely of 'time', but 'the time' suggests that he has a very specific sense of time in mind: that of the stage of God's purpose in salvation in which they were living. He has already alluded to this in the previous chapter in his exhortation, 'And whatever you do, in word or deed, do everything in the name of the Lord Jesus Christ' (3:17). It was not merely that, because of their Christian faith, Jesus Christ now coloured everything in life for these believers in Colossae; but that between the time of Christ's coming and the day of his return the world is living in a unique period of history. It is 'the time' of opportunity to hear the message of salvation through Christ. Hence Paul's urgency as he sets this new perspective on life before these people.

That thought carries through into the final exhortation in this section: 'Let your speech always be gracious, seasoned with salt, so that you may know how you ought to answer each person' (4:6). Given the whole thrust of what Paul has been saying in these verses about getting the gospel out to an unbelieving world, this is no vague generality. His reference to knowing 'how you ought to answer each person' really only makes sense in terms of what Peter elsewhere describes as giving 'the reason for the hope that is within you' (*1 Pet.* 3:15). That is, always being ready to bear witness to Christ.

If it is true that our entire conduct as Christians has a bearing on the message we convey to outsiders about our Saviour, then how much more our conversation – not just in terms of what we say directly as we share the gospel, but in our speech generally. It is all too easy for us to be very slick and professional in the way we present the message of Christ to unbelievers, only to contradict what we have said by the tone and content of our conversation generally. So our speech ought to be 'gracious' and 'seasoned with salt'.

It would seem that the graciousness Paul mentions points to the tone of what we say and how we say it. There is no place for harshness, arrogance, disdain or a patronizing or judgmental spirit in our speech. (Yet, if truth be told, such things come across too often in the way Christians address those who have yet to come to faith.) So too Paul's reference to 'salt' as the 'seasoning' in what we say, suggests flavour, appropriateness and 'edge'. In other words, our testimony to Christ as Saviour ought not to come across as bland and tasteless. Such is the weight of who he is and how great is the salvation he has secured that this is by far the most significant message the world has ever heard. Nothing is worse than when Christians make it sound boring and irrelevant.

It would be easy to overlook the importance of this little section in Paul's letter. He really is bringing all that he has been saying into sharp and practical focus. It is only as we get our heads and hearts around the things that really matter in life – in terms of God's dealings with our world through his Son – that we will indeed learn to pray, live and speak in a way that is shaped by those things that matter most.

17

You Are Not Alone!

Tychicus will tell you all about my activities. He is a beloved brother and faithful minister and fellow servant in the Lord. ⁸ I have sent him to you for this very purpose, that you may know how we are and that he may encourage your hearts, ⁹ and with him Onesimus, our faithful and beloved brother, who is one of you. They will tell you of everything that has taken place here. ¹⁰ Aristarchus my fellow prisoner greets you, and Mark the cousin of Barnabas (concerning whom you have received instructions – if he comes to you, welcome him), ¹¹ and Jesus who is called Justus. These are the only men of the circumcision among my fellow workers for the kingdom of God, and they have been a comfort to me. ¹² Epaphras, who is one of you, a servant of Christ Jesus, greets you, always struggling on your behalf in his prayers, that you may stand mature and fully assured in all the will of God. ¹³ For I bear him witness that he has worked hard for you and for those in Laodicea and in Hierapolis. ¹⁴ Luke the beloved physician greets you, as does Demas. ¹⁵ Give my greetings to the brothers at Laodicea, and to Nympha and the church in her house. ¹⁶ And when this letter has been read among you, have it also read in the church of the Laodiceans; and see that you also read the letter from Laodicea. ¹⁷ And say to Archippus, 'See that you fulfil the ministry that you have received in the Lord.' ¹⁸ I, Paul, write this greeting with my own hand. Remember my chains. Grace be with you. (Col. 4:7–18)

This closing section of Paul's letter to the Colossians presents us with a list of names – some of which are well known to us from other parts of the New Testament, others which are not. Paul mentions them all because they were clearly familiar to the Christians to whom he was writing. The problem for readers who were and are not part of that original congregation in Colossae is that it can feel more than a little odd to have them included in this way. It can be a bit like that feeling of being left out that comes when two people in a crowd start speaking about their own circle of friends which no one else in the room is part of.

It is not unusual for Paul to make mention of people in this way at the close of his letters. And, even though it might come across as just a convenient way of passing on news and greetings in a world where communications were much slower and less straightforward than is true of our own age of mass communication, there was much more going on. In the same way that the apostle was able to use the standard protocols of how to begin a letter in his day as a vehicle for the main body of what he wanted to say to its recipients, so too he uses some of those conventions in the way that he drew it to its close.

As we look at the names he mentions in these verses and the particular details he highlights in relation to these people two things become clear. Each of them in one way or another are connected to the church in Colossae and all of them are concerned about its needs. In other words, Paul was tactfully reminding these Christians to whom he was writing that they were not alone!

For any church as much as any Christian individually to go through a time of crisis in their life of faith can be an isolating as much as an unnerving experience. When the details of their troubles come to light, there is a very real temptation to feel as though their life – with all its struggles and failures – has been laid bare for all to see. Worse than that, there can be a horrible sensation of being all alone in a situation that no one else quite understands or appreciates. Paul's desire here especially is to show these people that this was not the case.

As he has been impressing on them literally from the opening verses of this letter, he wants them to realize that to be 'in Christ' (1:2) means far more than to be bound up with him in a private and personal relationship through saving faith, or even to be bound up in fellowship with other Christians in a local congregation; but to be part of the universal family of God. To be joined to Jesus is to be joined to every one of his blood-bought children through all the world and all of history. Putting names on some of those spiritual brothers and sisters for the Colossians helps them to put faces on that great fellowship to which they belong.

More than that, even in this closing section the apostle presses home the challenge he has been making all through his letter to the false teachers who had crept in among the Colossians and who were disseminating ideas about the Christian faith that were misguided and which had the effect of constructing an image of what it meant to be a Christian that was wrong. So, by connecting the names he mentions in this closing section in the way he does, Paul is quietly holding up a portrait of what genuine Christianity looks like.

Paul invites us into the closeness of these family ties as they relate to the particular situation that was affecting the church at Colossae at that time in a way that helps us to grasp its wider expression through the ages. It opens our eyes to the meaningful oneness we have in the church as the body of the Christ.

A FELLOWSHIP OF LOVE

As Paul goes through this list of names, it quickly becomes apparent that the relationship they share is anything but superficial. Not once, but three times he uses the adjective 'beloved' to describe several of them. Tychicus and Onesimus are both referred to as 'beloved brother' (4:7, 9) and Luke as 'the beloved physician' (4:14). These men could not have been more different in terms of their background and spheres of life and yet they had been bound together in the same bond of love through the Lord Jesus Christ. Tychicus was one of Paul's faithful travelling companions, Onesimus was the runaway slave on whose account the letter of Philemon was written and Luke was doctor who was responsible for writing the Gospel that bears his name as well as Acts. He too was a frequent companion of Paul on his missionary journeys.

Even though these men had virtually nothing in common that would have brought them into such a deep and affectionate bond of friendship in a different life, their shared relationship in Christ marked the beginning of a unique kind of friendship in him. Indeed, the sheer breadth of social standing represented in these three names in itself sent a signal to the Colossians who were being swayed by the notion of inner circles of privilege and importance within the family of faith. Here was living proof that Christ is no respecter of persons as he builds his church (3:11).

[127]

Another surprising name in this vein is the inclusion of 'Mark the cousin of Barnabas' (4:10). He was the John Mark who accompanied Paul and Barnabas on their first missionary journey (*Acts* 12:25), only to desert them when they got as far as Perga in Pamphylia (*Acts* 13:13). This in turn led to a major parting of the ways between Paul and Barnabas at the beginning of the second missionary journey (*Acts* 15:37-39). Given the seriousness of the disagreement that had arisen in that incident, it would not have been surprising if the apostle from that point onwards had chosen to quietly sideline him. But that is not the case. The Colossians had already received instructions about him which Paul here endorses by saying, 'if he comes to you, welcome him' (4:10). Such was the love that tied these brothers together that, despite past failures, there was genuine forgiveness and wholehearted restoration of relationships. This too would have sent quiet but powerful signals to the fellowship in Colossae which was suffering from strained relationships in its midst.

Another feature of the love that binds together the seemingly disparate list of names in these verses is the fact that it is expressed not only in kind words that are spoken but through the actions to which it led. In the case of Tychicus it was seen in his willingness to make a special trip to Colossae at Paul's behest to make sure that the church there was given a first-hand report on how the apostle was faring during his imprisonment. For Aristarchus (and Paul as well) it was in their willingness to suffer for the sake of Christ and the gospel. Mark and 'Jesus who is called Justus' – the only men among Paul's fellow workers who were 'of the circumcision' (that is, who had come to faith from a Jewish background) – had rallied to Paul to 'comfort' him in his harsh circumstances (4:10, 11). Here was love that made a very real difference to how these people lived for each other as much as for their Lord.

The hallmark of love that Jesus told his disciples was the ultimate badge of true discipleship (*John* 13:35) was stamped all over the lives of these people and it was a love that reached out to the believers in Colossae, despite the difficulties that had emerged in their church. That same love continues to be the mark of all members of God's true family down through the ages.

A FELLOWSHIP OF PRAYER

We have noted already how Paul emphasizes the importance of prayer in the life of the church generally and urges it upon the members of the church to whom he was writing (4:2-4), but here he holds up Epaphras as a model of what that looks like in practice.

The fact he punctuates his reference to Epaphras with the little note 'who is one of you' (4:12) shows that he in a very real sense is the living connector in the bond of love that joins the church in Colossae to the wider church of which it was a part. He may well have been the only person in the list of those Paul names who had a firsthand relationship with the congregation there; but as such his passion for these people was seen powerfully not just in what he prayed for them, but also in the way he prayed.

After conveying his greetings to the congregation, Paul says he is 'always struggling on your behalf in his prayers that you may stand mature and fully assured in all the will of God' (4:12). As we noted in an earlier chapter, the verb translated 'struggling' at this point is the same Greek word that gives us the English 'agonize' and the tense he uses makes it clear that this is no mere momentary spasm of anguish, but which has endured for at least as long as this man has known of the trouble in the church he had planted.

What is so striking in Paul's choice of word at this point is the fact that it is the same word that is used to describe Jesus' agonizing in prayer in the Garden of Gethsemane (*Luke* 22:44). The same kind of intensity that had poured out of Christ in his anticipation of the cross was mirrored in the praying of this man whose deepest longing was to see the blessings secured by Jesus' death brought to full fruition in the lives of his people. And as the very people for whom he was praying were allowed to catch a glimpse of how he prayed, that in itself would have spoken volumes as to how much they mattered to their spiritual father in the faith.

The fact that Paul goes on to say, 'For I bear him witness that he has worked hard for you and for those in Laodicea and in Hierapolis' (4:13), ties in with this. It was not merely that Epaphras' 'hands on' involvement in these places as a servant of the gospel had involved very real effort; but his 'behind the scenes' labour in prayer had been just as energetic and costly. And it is so often what a person invests away from the public gaze and recognition that says most about their devotion to God's people and his work.

So too as they listened to the content of his prayers – again so very much like those of a father who wants to see his children grow up into maturity, stability and usefulness – they saw themselves in the mirror of those prayers in a way that deepened their sense of need on the one hand, but that reminded of the One who alone could meet their need on the other.

Here again Paul was encouraging his readers to see that the relationships within the church are always three-dimensional. Even though they involve God's people's relating to one another on the horizontal plane, it is never in isolation from their relationship with God through Christ on the vertical plane.

A FELLOWSHIP IN CHRIST

We have already noted just how disparate this list of people Paul mentioned really was – Onesimus: a runaway slave, Mark: a failed missionary, Luke: a respected physician, and Nympha: only mentioned here and whose only claim to fame was the fact she was willing to let her house be used as a place of worship for the church, probably in Laodicea. What on earth did they have in common? The answer can only be, to use Paul's favoured expression, because they were all 'in Christ'. That was the language Paul had used at the beginning of his letter to the Colossians and that was the language that he had used throughout to show these Christians that what made them different was that they had been united to him as Saviour and Lord.

As news had spread about the embryonic church in Colossae it had become clear that they were not merely marked by their love for one another in their own particular church, but by the 'love that [they] had for all the saints' (1:4). This was another expression of the whole new web of relationships into which they had been brought through conversion. Even though in one sense there was no reason for them to have been interested in anyone else – Christian or otherwise – who was not from Colossae; their new relationship with Christ had literally opened a whole new horizon for them in terms of who 'their people' really were.

[130]

It is that extraordinary new dimension of life that is found through faith in Jesus Christ that becomes the note on which Paul draws this letter to its conclusion. He not only signs off with the words, 'I, Paul, write this greeting with my own hand' – most likely having literally taken the pen from the amanuensis, or scribe to whom he had been dictating these words – but blesses his readers by saying, 'Grace be with you.' (4:18).

All too often in Christian circles 'grace' is thought to be some kind of spiritual commodity – the rather abstract thought of 'God's unmerited favour'. That is indeed what it is, but it is anything but abstract. For Paul and for the other apostles, the embodiment of grace was found in the Person of the Lord Jesus Christ. As John was to record at the beginning of his Gospel, he was the One who came from the Father and was 'full of grace and truth' (*John* 1:14). So, for Paul to leave the Colossians with the benediction, 'Grace be with you', he was in effect saying 'The Lord Jesus Christ be with you!' What a great reminder to them and to us that in Christ we are never ever alone!

PHILEMON

Introduction to Philemon

Paul's little letter to Philemon is one of those often-overlooked gems of the Bible. Like some of the other single-chapter books such as Obadiah in the Old Testament and 3 John in the New, its brevity and perceived obscurity as to its main message have caused it to be neglected. So it is only when we take a closer look that we begin to appreciate why it is included in the canon of Holy Scripture as part of God's inspired and authoritative revelation.

Before we begin to look more closely at Paul's message in this mini-epistle, it would be helpful to fill in some of the background that surrounds its writing.

ITS CONNECTION WITH COLOSSIANS

One of the obvious questions to ask as we start looking at this letter (not least in the context of this commentary) is why it is linked with Paul's letter to the Colossians. Almost all commentaries on Philemon are appended to commentaries on Colossians. But why should this be, especially since these two letters are separated by five other of Paul's letters in the sequence of books in the New Testament?

Three major clues establish the connection for us. The first is the reference to Timothy in the opening verse of each of these letters. Both must have been written at a time when these two men were either travelling together, or – as is clear from another shared detail in the letters – when they were both in the same place at the same time. Since both letters indicate that Paul was writing from prison (*Col.* 4:3; *Philem.* 1), Timothy was at least staying close by for support during his time of incarceration.

The second link can be seen in the way Paul's prayer at the beginning of Philemon (*Philem.* 4-5) strongly echoes his prayer for the Colossians (*Col.* 1:3-4). Although this could be seen as circumstantial and no more than an example of Paul using similar language in different prayers for different situations, it would make sense to see it as Paul's thanksgiving for the Colossian church in general terms being offered for one of its members specifically. This in turn feeds through into the fact that a number of the principles Paul had set out by way of broad instruction in the Colossian letter – in particular to slaves and their masters (*Col.* 4:1) – are developed in detail in Philemon.

The third major clue that ties these two letters together is the overlap of names associated with both. Paul refers not only to Tychicus as the person he is sending to Colossae (*Col.* 4:7-8) – quite probably as the courier who would deliver the letter – but also to Onesimus as his travelling companion (*Col.* 4:9). Onesimus is the main reason for Paul's writing to Philemon and it is clear that he too was being sent by Paul back to Philemon as his rightful owner (*Philem.* 12). As well as this, it is not hard to see that the same people who send their greetings at the end of the Colossian letter – Epaphras, Mark, Aristarchus, Demas, Luke and Archippus – are also mentioned in Philemon (*Philem.* 2, 23-25).

These little details do more than merely establish a circumstantial connection between these two letters, in that they happened to be written around the same time and were sent to the same general locality; but show that their respective messages are closely related as well.

DATE AND PLACE OF WRITING

Given what we have said already about the connections that tie Colossians and Philemon together, the date and location from which both were written are almost certainly the same. In light of what was noted in the Introduction to Colossians, this dates Philemon sometime around A.D. 60 during Paul's first imprisonment in Rome. As we noted before, this was an imprisonment which was more akin to house arrest, since the apostle enjoyed significant visitation rights from all kinds of people who wished to see him. This would help to explain why Onesimus, the slave whose conduct was the catalyst for this letter's being written, would have had access to Paul at that time.

In more recent studies of this letter, some scholars have suggested Ephesus as an alternative setting from which Paul wrote. The main assumption behind this being the fact that if Onesimus had run away from his master, Philemon, it would have been more likely for him to have looked for refuge in a city like Ephesus 120 miles away rather than the capital of the Empire almost 1,000 miles away. However, even those who have put forward this suggestion have acknowledged that it raises as many questions as it attempts to answer.

RECIPIENT AND KEY CONCERNS

The name that identifies this letter has been widely regarded as settling the issue of to whom the letter was addressed: something that its opening words seem to confirm. However, on closer inspection, Philemon is not the only addressee in what Paul says. Apphia, Archippus and 'the church that meets at your [probably Philemon's] house' are also included. The inclusion of a wider audience is further reinforced by the fact that although Paul uses 'you' in its singular form for most of what he says, he also uses the second person plural at the beginning and end of the letter, most notably when he speaks about his desire to visit at some point in the future (*Philem.* 22).

This helps us to understand to some extent why a letter which on face value appears to be private and personal has been included in the Bible for the benefit of the church. Even though it was indeed very specific to one man and a particular situation he was facing, that one man could not be isolated from the church family of which he was a part.

Different attempts have been made to piece together the clues from the text of this letter and reconstruct the precise problem that led to its being written. Not all of them are as clear as has often been made out; but without question they focus on a slave called Onesimus who has run away from his master, Philemon, and has come into contact with the apostle Paul. Through him he heard the gospel and was brought to faith in Jesus Christ. The essence of Paul's concern seems to crystallize when Paul says to Philemon,

'So if you consider me your partner, receive him as you would receive me' (*Philem.* 17). The apostle was making this request, not by way of command, but, rather, as an expression of the fellowship of the gospel that joined a Christian slave-owner to his recently converted slave.

As we have hinted already, although the substance of this matter concerns a private issue between Paul, Philemon and Onesimus, there are many reasons to see the horizons of the letter as being much broader, not just for the church to which Philemon belonged, but to the church of all ages.

RELEVANCE TO THE CHURCH TODAY

Given not only the private nature of this correspondence between Paul and Philemon, but more so the very distinctive situation it addressed, we might be left wondering what it is meant to teach the church today. In many parts of the world slavery has been eradicated (though it is still a far bigger social evil than many realize), so how can it be of benefit to the church in general?

At one level it is significant that Paul does not present Philemon with a manifesto for social reform. Slavery was a major component of the social and economic world in the Roman Empire and was a much more complex institution than many people today appreciate. If the apostle and with him the early church had chosen to mount a major campaign for its abolition, it would have created a huge distraction to why the church exists and what its primary focus is: namely, the gospel. In that sense, even though the church through the ages was to become a key player in the movement to abolish slavery, social reform has not been its primary calling.

When we look more closely at how the issue of slavery, with its many ramifications, is handled in this letter, we see how much it is impacted by the gospel in a way that not merely affects slaves and their owners, but the wider church and indeed society at large as well. Recognizing this in what Paul says in this letter opens up a whole new vista to its relevance to the church through the ages.

I

A Greeting, a Prayer, and the Key to the Letter

Paul, a prisoner for Christ Jesus, and Timothy our brother, To Phile-
mon our beloved fellow worker ²and Apphia our sister and Archippus
our fellow soldier, and the church in your house: ³Grace to you and
peace from God our Father and the Lord Jesus Christ. ⁴I thank my
God always when I remember you in my prayers, ⁵because I hear of
your love and of the faith that you have toward the Lord Jesus and
for all the saints, ⁶and I pray that the sharing of your faith may
become effective for the full knowledge of every good thing that is in
us for the sake of Christ. ⁷For I have derived much joy and comfort
from your love, my brother, because the hearts of the saints have been
refreshed through you. (Philem. 1-7)

It is always fascinating to see the extent to which the circumstances surrounding a letter shape and mould not only what it
says, but how its message is conveyed. That comes across in all
of Paul's letters and it comes across here in what he has to say to
Philemon.

From the very start in its opening greeting and prayer, we begin
to sense that the dimensions of the problem addressed in the letter
are actually much greater than we might first imagine. Although,
as we shall quickly see when we get into the main body of the letter,
it concerns a very specific issue – the relationship between a slave
and his owner – in reality its horizons are much larger. The two
lives immediately involved touch and are touched by many other
lives and are shaped ultimately by God himself.

In many ways this only becomes clear after a second or third
reading of the letter, but when we read its beginning in light of
all that follows, we cannot help but see that the greeting and the

opening thanksgiving and prayer are deeply coloured by all that
Paul goes on to say.

FROM WHOM AND TO WHOM AND WHY

Paul was well acquainted with the protocols of letter-writing in
his day. Not only was he well-educated as a Jew, he also had the
privilege of being a Roman citizen and was very much aware of the
social conventions and expectations of the time. All his letters, as
much as the record of his travels around the Mediterranean world,
show how sensitive he is to the customs and culture of that era and
to particular details in how they affected the people he dealt with.

So here, dealing with the highly sensitive issue of a slave who
has seriously disrespected his owner and master, he is creatively
careful in how he chooses his words. Philemon is one of only a
few of Paul's letters in which he does not identify himself from
the outset as an 'apostle'. Instead, here he describes himself as 'a
prisoner for Christ Jesus' (*Philem.* 1).

His decision not to flag up his apostolic credentials may simply
be because he is writing primarily to a friend in a somewhat private
capacity. More likely it is because he deliberately wants to distance
himself from seeming coercive in what he has to say. Later on in
the letter he will make it plain that he wants Philemon to accede to
his request, not because he has to, but because Paul's appeal is 'for
love's sake' (*Philem.* 9) and the desired response should not be 'by
compulsion, but of your own free will' (*Philem.* 14).

Add to this the fact that Paul describes himself as a 'prisoner for
Christ Jesus' or, 'of Christ Jesus' and we see something about the
way Paul is conveying his request. It isn't just that he has, from a
human perspective, been detained at Caesar's pleasure; but because
of his allegiance to Christ and the gospel. Such was the apostle's
devotion to the gospel that he was willing to suffer major personal
loss for the sake of the gospel. That is the broader principle that is
true for all believers and which underlies all he will go on to say to
his brother in Christ in what follows.

Philemon is not the only name that appears in the address line
of this letter. Apphia and Archippus are also mentioned. Although
the former is referred to as 'our sister', many commentators believe
that she may well have been Philemon's wife. Likewise, Archippus,

mentioned in relation to the work he was doing in Colossians (*Col.* 4:17), is described as 'our fellow soldier'. The inclusion of his name in the greeting section of Philemon may also indicate that he belongs to Philemon's household and may, as many think, even have been his son.

The reference to 'the church in your house' broadens the scope of what Paul is saying even further. There are good grammatical reasons for seeing the 'your' in this clause as referring to Philemon and if what has been suggested above regarding his relationship with Apphia and Archippus, then it helps us to understand why a Christian congregation is being allowed to eavesdrop on what the apostle is saying to their host family. It is not just that their meeting under the same roof as their benefactors would have led to their knowing about the Onesimus affair, but more than that, the fact that they belonged to the same spiritual family would have meant that the concern of Philemon's family was very much their concern as well.

Whatever the full picture may be, there is enough in this opening to show that the people named along with Philemon were to varying degrees affected by the issues Paul needed to address with him. As to what those issues were, the details will soon become clear in what the apostle goes on to say; but, as is the case in nearly all his other letters, Paul nuances what is a fairly standard greeting in letter-writing convention of his day to pave the way for what his readers need to hear.

As he writes into a situation in which discord has entered a relationship and justice demands certain actions in face of what has happened, he says, 'Grace to you and peace from God our Father and the Lord Jesus Christ' (*Philem.* 3). Before he speaks about the problems facing Philemon in his relationship with Onesimus, he speaks about God's solution to the problem he faces in relationship with all men. In that relationship there is also discord because of our human rebellion against God and there too God's justice has certain demands that cannot be ignored. But the glory of the gospel is that through the saving work of our Lord Jesus Christ, divine justice has been satisfied and God is able to deal with us on the basis of grace, thus establishing peace where once there was hostility.

GOOD REASON TO BE THANKFUL

We have noted already in the Introduction that Paul's prayer of thanksgiving for Philemon carries a strong echo of his prayer for the church in Colossae generally (*Col.* 1:3-4). Paul tells Philemon that his reputation has gone before him. Even though the two men were apparently already well acquainted, the apostle says, 'I hear of your love and of the faith that you have towards the Lord Jesus and all the saints' (*Philem.* 5).

As we read that statement, one difficulty seems to leap off the page, at least with the English translation of what Paul is saying. Whereas we can appreciate the reference to Philemon's love for both the Lord Jesus and all the saints, it is hard to see how the 'faith' he has could be towards both the Lord and his people at the same time. Different translators and commentators have offered suggestions as to how that tension can be relieved, but the most plausible would seem to be that Paul is using a grammatical construction in the way his sentence is ordered in the Greek that has the effect of pairing the reference to 'love' with 'all the saints' and 'faith' with 'the Lord Jesus'. This is not only more in keeping with the way Paul uses similar language in his other letters, but it also makes the best sense of the words he uses here.

When we clarify that ambiguity, we can well appreciate why the apostle takes particular note of these two characteristics of his friend Philemon, especially as they have shaped his reputation more widely in the Christian community and beyond. In line with what Jesus himself told his disciples in the Upper Room on the eve of his crucifixion, love for one another as Christians would be the most visible and telling badge of discipleship the church could ever have (*John* 13:35). And when it is seen – especially, as was the case with Philemon, with such consistency – it can only be understood in light of a Christian's relationship with Jesus Christ through faith.

So, before Paul even gets to the main point of why he is writing to Philemon, he shares with him his gratitude to God for the evidence of the kind of gracious spirit towards others that Paul knows he can appeal to on behalf of Onesimus.

Some commentaries suggest that in this early part of the letter Paul is following a recognized pattern of writing this kind of letter in which he deliberately tries to curry favour with Philemon to 'soften him up' for the big request he wants to make of him. Whereas there may indeed be similarities of style in the form of writing Paul uses here, it would be disingenuous to think that the apostle would use something like that to make such a serious appeal to a fellow Christian – especially to one he clearly regarded as a friend.

It makes much more sense and is far more in keeping with what Paul says in all his letters to see this opening word of thanksgiving – which is after all directed towards God and not Philemon – as an expression of real confidence that his friend will hear his request and respond with Christian grace. Even though he is asking for something that lies outside the bounds of human expectation, it is not beyond the limits of what God can enable his people to do.

THE KEY TO ALL THAT FOLLOWS

All this leads into a verse that is critical to all that follows. It is not an easy verse to translate, but when we begin to get the sense of what Paul is saying, we are then able to appreciate more fully what lies at the heart of Paul's prayer.

The key words in this verse are translated (at least by the ESV) as 'sharing' and 'faith'. The big question that hovers over them is 'How are they connected?' The sense conveyed by the way they are put together in the ESV is that Philemon's 'faith' – in the sense of 'life of faith' – is not something private and personal, but something that is to be shared with others in the household of faith. That is certainly true and it goes a long way to capturing what lies at the heart of the apostle's prayer at this point. It is possible, however, to sharpen up our view of what Paul is expressing here.

The word translated 'sharing' is the Greek word *koinonia* – a word that is often translated 'fellowship'. It carries the sense, at least almost always in the way that Paul uses it, of the dynamic relationship established between all God's people collectively because of their relationship with him personally through Jesus Christ. So, if we as Christians are being changed in our lives individually through our fellowship with Christ, then that change must of necessity spill over into how we relate to our fellow Christians.

When we look at this verse through that lens then it sharpens our understanding of what Paul is praying for on behalf of his friend, Philemon. In particular, it helps us to see the web of connections Paul has in mind as he offers this prayer. In terms of the kind of action for which Paul is praying, the apostle wants Philemon to relate to all his fellow believers – including Onesimus – in a way that is shaped by his faith in Jesus Christ. As Philemon sees that prayer being answered by finding help from God to behave towards a slave in a way that was totally counter-cultural in that time, Paul also prays that his action would become 'effective' towards his spiritual progress. The kind of progress Paul describes as being 'for the full knowledge of every good thing that is in us for the sake of Christ'.

It is hard to convey the sheer weight and magnitude of the point Paul is making in this verse; but the essence of it is this. If Philemon in particular (and Christians in general) can have the faith and the courage to behave towards others – even the most unlikely people – out of allegiance to Christ instead of culture, then the ramifications are enormous. At a personal level, we as believers come to experience firsthand just how good the 'good things' are that we have in Jesus Christ. More widely this is experienced by the entire family of God, because they are 'in us' collectively and not just the private preserve of a few. This in turn can only enhance the church's witness to Christ and his gospel because it is all done, not for our own sake, or for the sake of social norms and expectations, but 'for the sake of Christ'.

Breath-taking and all as this statement may have sounded to Philemon; Paul knew that it really wasn't new to him. Hence he goes on to speak of the way he himself, as well as the hearts of all the saints who knew this man, had been 'refreshed' through his actions already. Such had been his 'love' – as expressed within the Christian community – that it was not only plain to see by all, but it had become a source of 'joy and comfort' to the apostle.

It is that extraordinary pleasure of seeing the gospel do its work in people's lives – not just in the way that the Lord Jesus transforms sinners in their lives individually, but that he does so in the shared life we enjoy as his people in the church.

2

An Appeal, an Argument, and their Underlying Motive

Accordingly, though I am bold enough in Christ to command you to do what is required, ^{9} yet for love's sake I prefer to appeal to you – I, Paul, an old man and now a prisoner also for Christ Jesus – ^{10} I appeal to you for my child, Onesimus, whose father I became in my imprisonment. ^{11} (Formerly he was useless to you, but now he is indeed useful to you and to me.) ^{12} I am sending him back to you, sending my very heart. ^{13} I would have been glad to keep him with me, in order that he might serve me on your behalf during my imprisonment for the gospel, ^{14} but I preferred to do nothing without your consent in order that your goodness might not be by compulsion but of your own accord. ^{15} For this perhaps is why he was parted from you for a while, that you might have him back forever, ^{16} no longer as a slave but more than a slave, as a beloved brother – especially to me, but how much more to you, both in the flesh and in the Lord. (Philem. 8-16)

These verses take us into the main body of Paul's message to Philemon. Although, as was said in the introductory comments, the actual appeal or request that lies at the heart of the letter is not made until verse 17, it is significant that even in this section the apostle is building his case in support of that request. As a general principle, Paul does not tell, or even ask Christians to do something without first setting out the reasons not only as to why they should do them morally, but what actually enables them to do so in terms of their spiritual resources.

Paul's approach is completely in line with the way God speaks throughout the Bible as a whole. The Scriptures never present commands without first of all spelling out what God has done through salvation to enable his people to fulfil those commands.

[143]

Or, as someone once said, 'There are no unplugged imperatives in the Bible!'

Paul is leading up to a request that would weigh heavily on Philemon for all kinds of reasons; but the apostle is careful to marshal and present reasons for him to accede to that request that carry far more weight than the request itself.

His approach is freighted with pastoral wisdom. On the one hand Paul shows how much he is aware of that human instinct – one that lingers on in a person's life, even after he, or she has become a Christian – to measure everything from 'self' as the central reference point. It is the default position of the sin that continues to indwell us even as the children of God. Paul testifies to his own struggle with this tendency in Romans 7. So his approach comes with the kind of sensitivity that is designed to defuse this destructive element in our nature.

On the other hand, and even more significantly, the apostle makes the case for Philemon to hear his appeal and see it from the broader perspective of what God is doing in the lives of other Christians in particular – not least in the life of Paul himself – but also in the life of church at large. All this builds on the foundation of what he has given thanks for and prayed about in the preceding verses.

As we follow through the build-up in Paul's argument and appreciate the contours of his reasoning, we begin to see not only how God was dealing with Philemon, but how he continues to deal with all his children.

AN APPEAL ARISING OF LOVE

Paul moves from acknowledging Philemon's love for others in the previous verse to appealing for a further display of that love in what follows by using the word 'accordingly' (*Philem.* 8) as a connector. In other words, he is not calling on his friend to show something towards this one believer, Onesimus, that he has not already shown to other believers in other contexts.

He reinforces this approach by making it clear that even though, as an apostle, he had the authority to simply command Philemon to take his delinquent slave back into his household, instead he appeals to him to do so 'for love's sake' (*Philem.* 9). The reference to 'love' in light of the wider context would seem to point back to the idea of koinonia or 'sharing of your faith' (*Philem.* 6). He is subtly, but with a different kind of boldness, reminding his slave-owner friend that the dynamic of love runs deep within the family of God and is not limited by class or status.

This line of reasoning should give pause for thought to all Christians in all kinds of life situations. From parents and the way they raise their children, to those in authority in work or governments and the way they direct those who are under them, to church leaders and the way they exercise oversight in their congregations. The way we encourage others to 'do what is required' (*Philem.* 8) – whatever that might be – can never be through cold commands by themselves.

The point is pressed home by the way Paul goes on to describe himself. Even though he was indeed an apostle, he was now 'an old man', more than that, he was an old man who was 'now a prisoner for Christ Jesus' (*Philem.* 9). As he himself had throughout his life of faith walked the very path he was exhorting Philemon to walk, it had cost him dearly from a human point of view, but he had not wavered in accepting that cost, even in the face of imprisonment.

It is perhaps ironic that the beauty and the power of love are most visible, not in the happy circumstances and choices of life to which we are easily drawn, but in the painful circumstances and hard choices that we face. That was visible to all in the life of the ageing apostle and he was now asking that it might be seen also in the life and conduct of his friend from Colossae.

AN ARGUMENT BASED ON THE POWER OF THE GOSPEL

Paul takes his argument to the next level as he goes on to name the person on whose behalf he is making his appeal and the circumstances that lie behind it. But before naming him, he refers to him as 'my child...whose father I became in my imprisonment' (*Philem.* 10). He is, of course, Onesimus – the slave whose name would have leapt off the page as Philemon read this letter – but he was not the same Onesimus who had absconded from Philemon's household at some point in the past.

Paul uses the language of 'child' and 'father' in the spiritual sense of the part he had played in this man's coming to faith in the Lord Jesus Christ. He uses similar language elsewhere, notably in relation to Timothy who he describes as his 'true son in the faith' (*1 Tim.* 1:2). Although he was clearly neither his biological father, or even his adoptive father, he had very likely become his 'father in the faith' through his involvement with this young man's conversion when they first met in Timothy's hometown of Lystra.

So, filling in the gaps in what Paul is saying here, it would seem that during Paul's imprisonment in Rome, he somehow came across this runaway slave. In the course of their conversations and getting to know each other, Onesimus became a Christian and their relationship took on a whole new dimension. Some have speculated that, given Paul's prior friendship with Onesimus' master, Philemon, he may well have heard about Paul and deliberately sought him out in Rome, seeking help under his present circumstances. He had perhaps heard the apostle's name being mentioned in his old household and had been impressed by how much he obviously meant to Philemon and his family and so, when he had no-one else to turn to in Rome, he had turned to Paul, only to discover that he really needed to turn to Christ.

Regardless of whether or not the details reflect the actual circumstances of Onesimus' conversion, the bottom line is the same. He heard the gospel from Paul and through the power of that gospel he came to faith and he became a new man.

It is, of course, that same gospel which has proved that it still is 'the power of God for salvation' (*Rom.* 1:16) in countless lives through the ages. From alcoholics to adulterers, respectable businessmen to reckless teenagers, it is more than able to take lives that have been ruined by sin and make them new through the saving work of Jesus Christ.

Paul goes on to throw the spotlight on just how new this slave has become. Using a three-way play on words in the Greek he says of Onesimus (whose name means 'useful'), 'Formerly he was useless to you, but now he is indeed useful to you and to me' (*Philem.* 11). When this slave had first come to the apostle and told him his story, Paul would have known only too well what this would have looked like through Philemon's eyes. Onesimus was an investment gone wrong. Not only did he represent a financial loss in the sense of what he had cost Philemon in the slave market, but he now represented a potentially huge loss of face if he were to return without being severely punished for what he had done.

However, as Paul had not only observed the genuineness of his newfound faith in Christ, but had also begun to see a whole new attitude and willingness to be useful as he looked after the needs of Paul in prison, he could see that had truly experienced a change of heart and could contemplate sending him back to his master with confidence.

It was clearly no small thing for Paul to take this step. As he speaks of sending Onesimus back to Philemon, he says it was like 'sending my very heart' (*Philem.* 12) – such was the closeness between the apostle and this new convert that it was a wrench to him to even think of losing him. Indeed he goes on to say that he would have been glad to keep him in Rome because of the service he was rendering to him there (*Philem.* 13). Nevertheless, he makes it clear to Onesimus' rightful owner, 'but I preferred to do nothing without your consent in order that your goodness might not be by compulsion but of your own free will' (*Philem.* 14).

Some have taken Paul's reference to 'goodness' there as a subtle hint that he would love Philemon to either send Onesimus back to Rome in order for him to continue working with Paul, or perhaps even grant this slave his freedom so that he could return to the apostle as a freedman. That is certainly a possible interpretation of what Paul is saying here; but equally it could simply be a reinforcement of what Paul has said already about Philemon only receiving Onesimus back if he is indeed willing to do so, recognizing that this once useless slave now, in Christ, possessed a usefulness he never had before.

As we think of the place of Philemon in the wider body of the books of the Bible, there is perhaps an even bigger play on words unfolding here. The fact that all of us as human beings, who by nature are worse than runaway slaves, are also by nature 'useless' to God; but we too can become 'useful' to him when we are restored to our rightful Lord and Master. And this, not merely because he is our Creator God, but because he has been willing to redeem us

– 'buy us back' – at extraordinary cost through the death of his Son on the cross.

The power of the gospel was a compelling reason for Philemon to see the return of Onesimus in an altogether different light.

A MOTIVE THAT IS LINKED TO THE PURPOSES OF GOD

Paul adds one further strand to his argument for Philemon to receive his slave with mercy and kindness: one that ties in to the higher purposes of God unfolding in this particular set of circumstances. He speaks of 'why he was parted from you' (*Philem.* 15), using a passive verb form that points beyond Onesimus' own decision to part company with his master, to the providence of God that was at work in and around as well as over and above one man's choices in life.

It brings us into a strand of teaching about God that runs all the way through the Bible. Namely, the fact that God not only created the world and universe, but that he is also intimately involved in providing for and governing the affairs of his creation through his providential care. It comes into sharp focus in face of the bad things that happen in the world in the story of Joseph in Genesis. Despite Joseph's own foolishness and his brothers' wickedness towards him (all of which led to years of misery for him), he himself is able to say to his brothers years later, 'As for you, you meant evil against me, but God meant it for good...' (*Gen.* 50:20). So for Onesimus: despite whatever warped motives lay behind his actions – even as someone who was not yet a Christian – God had a higher purpose for good that he was working out.

When Paul says that part of this purpose was that Philemon 'might have him back forever, no longer as a slave, but more than a slave, as a beloved brother...' (*Philem.* 15-16), he is encouraging his friend to see Onesimus' return in a different light. The fact that he was coming back as a member of the household of faith meant that he should be received back into his master's household in a different way. He had already endeared himself to Paul as a brother in the Lord and Paul was confident that he would prove to be the same as he went back to Philemon no longer merely in the 'flesh' relationship that once had bound them to each other as master and slave; but now in their newfound relationship 'in the Lord'.

In none of this was Paul either demanding or even implying that Philemon ought to grant Onesimus his freedom, but rather that he should recognize their relationship had been radically and eternally altered through the gospel and through the wise and loving purposes of the Sovereign Lord himself.

All this should give us pause for thought as we consider our own different sets of relationships in which we find ourselves. It is all too easy for us to view them and seek to direct them merely from a human point of view and with our own agenda in mind. If we are Christians, we need to reckon on the fact that there is always an unseen third party in every relationship we have: the God who directs all things for his own good pleasure, but also for his people's good (*Rom.* 8:28).

3

The Big Request and Its Even Bigger Horizons

*So if you consider me your partner, receive him as you would receive
me. [18] If he has wronged you at all, or owes you anything, charge that
to my account. [19] I, Paul, write this with my own hand: I will repay it
– to say nothing of your owing me even your own self. [20] Yes, brother,
I want some benefit from you in the Lord. Refresh my heart in Christ.
[21] Confident of your obedience, I write to you, knowing that you will
do even more than I say. [22] At the same time, prepare a guest room for
me, for I am hoping that through your prayers I will be graciously
given to you. [23] Epaphras, my fellow prisoner in Christ Jesus, sends
greetings to you, [24] and so do Mark, Aristarchus, Demas, and Luke,
my fellow workers. [25] The grace of the Lord Jesus Christ be with your
spirit.* (Philem. 17-25)

Everything Paul has been saying up to this point in this letter reaches its great crescendo in the big request he now lays
before his friend: a request which in many ways marked a water-
shed in their relationship.

It is perhaps hard for us because of our cultural and historical distance from the world in which Paul and Philemon lived, to
appreciate the magnitude of what the apostle was asking of his
friend. Philemon's family, neighbours and associates would have
been watching keenly to see what he would do with this recalci-
trant slave when he turned up at his master's door after having
been away for a significant length of time. Whatever his reaction
was, it was bound to have an impact on the way he was viewed by
his community. It would be no small thing to respond positively to
the request Paul was making.

Then again, throughout history and in all kinds of cultures,
Christians have found themselves facing similar challenges again

and again. Social and cultural norms place their own expectations on us to respond to particular situations in ways that are seen to uphold those norms, regardless of whether or not they have any divine warrant. Our great challenge as Christians is to have the courage to react, not in ways that keep our communities happy, but in a way that honours God.

For us, it will almost certainly not be the question of what should we do with a runaway slave, but it could quite possibly be, what should we do with a spouse who has cheated on us, a neighbour who has slandered us, or a business partner who has deceived us. How a person who is not a Christian might react is one thing, as they try to save face before a watching world; but how a Christian reacts is bound to be different, because they are being watched not just by those around them in the world, but by God as he watches us from heaven.

As Paul draws this little letter to its conclusion it is not only his big request that looms large in all he has to say, but the even bigger horizons against which it is set. We need to look at them more closely as we round off our study of what this letter is all about.

THE ONE RELATIONSHIP THAT TRANSFORMS ALL OTHER RELATIONSHIPS

Paul not only asks Philemon to do what in many ways was the culturally unthinkable thing to do, he asks him to go beyond that and 'receive him [Onesimus] as you would receive me' (*Philem.* 17). In other words, that he would accord this delinquent member of his household the same welcome and acceptance as he would have shown to the apostle himself.

The fact that Paul qualifies this request with the caveat, 'if you consider me your partner' serves only to intensify the weight of what he is saying. Even though most English Bible versions choose the word 'partner' to translate what Paul is saying here, it can easily miss the nuance of what Paul is conveying. The Greek word behind it is *koinonos* – clearly an echo of the word *koinonia* which Paul has already used (*Philem.* 6) – and it is almost certainly being used to refer to the partnership in the gospel which Paul and Philemon shared. So he is weighting his appeal with a reminder of just how deep his relationship went with Philemon.

The full depth and significance of that relationship are articulated explicitly at the end of this paragraph where the apostle says, 'Yes, brother, I want some benefit from you in the Lord. Refresh my soul in Christ' (*Philem.* 20). The 'in the Lord' and 'in Christ' phrases are Paul's standard way of referring to the one supreme relationship that shapes and moulds all others. Because these two men were bound up in the same bundle on life as Christ in salvation, then their personal life and conduct had to be transformed through him.

All this helps to explain the verses in between – why Paul is able to say on the one hand that if Onesimus has wronged Philemon or owes him anything, he himself would cover the costs. While in his very next breath he could also say directly to Philemon that he owes him his own life (*Philem.* 18-19). It would appear that Paul is making a veiled reference to the role he had played personally in Philemon's becoming a Christian.

In all of this the point the apostle is putting across is the fact that if we are Christians, our relationship with Christ, by definition, has an unbelievably far-reaching effect on how we relate to everyone and everything else in life.

THE CONFIDENCE THAT UNDERLIES THE BIG REQUEST

It would be tempting to think Paul was taking a huge risk in making this kind of request in these particular circumstances. Assuming that Philemon was a man of sufficient means to be able and willing to provide accommodation (and presumably other benefits) for the church that was meeting in his house, to hear what Paul was asking might be enough to alienate him, not just from the apostle, but potentially make him take a step back from his Christian involvement. That being the level of risk, no-one in his day would have been surprised if Paul had simply ignored this slave's plight and had seen him as expendable for the sake of Philemon's support for the church. But Paul does not reason that way.

Indeed, Paul does not waver for a moment in his anticipation of his friend and brother's response, but says, 'Confident of your obedience, I write to you knowing that you will do even more than I say' (*Philem.* 21). He has just exhorted Philemon with the words,

'Refresh my soul in Christ' (*Philem.* 20). In so doing he was picking up on what he had already given thanks for in the life of this man as he has observed the extent to which 'the hearts of the saints have been refreshed' through him (*Philem.* 7). That is, even though Philemon's actions had been a blessing to unnamed Christians generally, without realizing it, his love had become a source of 'joy and comfort' to the apostle Paul himself. Philemon already had an existing track record of the love and grace of Christ being shared with others through his life and actions and the apostle had no reason to doubt that his response to Onesimus' return would in any way deviate from it.

The underlying reason for this, of course, is not Paul's confidence in Philemon, but rather in Christ and in the power of the gospel. Where the gospel is doing its work in people's lives we can have every confidence that it will genuinely change them and enable them to speak and act in a way that reflects the grace and beauty of Christ in their dealings with others.

Paul rounds off this main section of his letter with an appended request for Philemon to prepare a guest room for him in anticipation of his being able to visit Colossae in person pending his release from prison (*Philem.* 22). That in itself says it all in terms of the response he expected Philemon to give to the letter as a whole.

THE GRACE THAT MAKES ALL THE DIFFERENCE IN LIFE

The letter ends with references to greetings and grace. The greetings come from almost the very same people who have asked to be remembered to the wider church in the Colossian letter – a little detail that demonstrates the depth and scope of the web of relationships that had come about through the gospel in the ancient world. People who were otherwise disconnected in life had become connected in Christ and they took every opportunity to express their love and concern for their fellow Christians, wherever they were and whatever their circumstances in life.

It is but another example of the koinonia fellowship that Paul not only mentions here, but that is one of the defining marks of what the church has been since its earliest days after the Day of Pentecost (*Acts* 2:42). It is the kind of fellowship and concern that ought to characterize the church through the ages – not just within the life of individual congregations, but which also embraces fellow-Christians all over the world and in every kind of situation.

As Paul signs off his letter with words of blessing, 'The grace of the Lord Jesus Christ be with your spirit' (*Philem.* 25), he is doing much more than just observing the protocols of letter-writing of the day. One only has to compare and contrast the apostle's precise choice of wording for such benedictions at the close of his other letters to realize that they are frequently customized to reinforce the individual message of those letters.

So here, in a letter that has focused on the desire for a Christian brother to show grace to someone who had caused serious offence to him, but who now himself was a brother in the Lord, Paul shows one last time how and why that should be the case. Philemon's ability to show Christlike grace to Philemon was wrapped up in the fact that he himself had not only received the grace of Christ at his conversion, but he was in daily need of that grace throughout his Christian experience.

The same is true for every Christian in every age. No matter what our personal circumstances and challenges of life may be the words of Robert Robinson's hymn ring true for us all. In a strange way they provide a fitting summary of all that Paul was saying to Philemon and had surely taught Onesimus in his newfound faith.

> O to grace how great a debtor
> Daily I'm constrained to be!
> Let Thy goodness, like a fetter,
> Bind my wandering heart to Thee.
> Prone to wander, Lord, I feel it,
> Prone to leave the God I love;
> Here's my heart, O take and seal it,
> Seal it for Thy courts above.

Group Study Guide

SCHEME FOR GROUP BIBLE STUDY ON COLOSSIANS
(Covering 13 weeks)

STUDY	STUDY PASSAGE	COMMENTARY CHAPTERS
1	Colossians 1:1-8	1–2
2	Colossians 1:9-14	3
3	Colossians 1:15-23	4–5
4	Colossians 1:24-2.5	6–7
5	Colossians 2:6-15	8–9
6	Colossians 2:16-19	10
7	Colossians 2:20-23	11
8	Colossians 3:1-4	12
9	Colossians 3:5-11	13
10	Colossians 3:12-17	14
11	Colossians 3:18-4.1	15
12	Colossians 4:2-6	16
13	Colossians 4:7-18	17

SCHEME FOR GROUP BIBLE STUDY ON PHILEMON
(Covering 1 week)

STUDY	STUDY PASSAGE	COMMENTARY CHAPTERS
1	Philemon	*Philemon sections* 1-3

[157]

This Study Guide has been prepared for group Bible study, but it can also be used individually. Those who use it on their own may find it helpful to keep a note of their responses in a notebook.

The way in which group Bible studies are led can greatly enhance their value. A well-conducted study will appear as though it has been easy to lead, but that is usually because the leader has worked hard and planned well. Clear aims are essential.

AIMS

In all Bible study, individual or corporate, we have several aims:

1. To gain an understanding of the original meaning of the particular passage of Scripture;

2. To apply this to ourselves and our own situation;

3. To develop some specific ways of putting the biblical teaching into practice.

2 Timothy 3:16–17 provides a helpful structure. Paul says that Scripture is useful for:

(i) teaching us;

(ii) rebuking us;

(iii) correcting, or changing us;

(iv) training us in righteousness.

Consequently, in studying any passage of Scripture, we should always have in mind these questions:

• What does this passage teach us (about God, ourselves, etc.)?

• Does it rebuke us in some way?

• How can its teaching transform us?

• What equipment does it give us for serving Christ?

In fact, these four questions alone would provide a safe guide in any Bible study.

PRINCIPLES

In group Bible study we meet in order to learn about God's Word and ways 'with all the saints' (*Eph.* 3:18). But our own experience, as well as Scripture, tells us that the saints are not always what they *are* called to be in every situation – including group Bible study! Leaders ordinarily have to work hard and prepare well if the work of the group is to be spiritually profitable. The following guidelines for leaders may help to make this a reality.

Preparation:

1. Study and understand the passage yourself. The better prepared and more sure of the direction of the study you are, the more likely it is that the group will have a beneficial and enjoyable study. Ask: What are the main things this passage is saying? How can this be made clear? This is not the same question as the more common 'What does this passage "say to you"?', which expects a reaction rather than an exposition of the passage. Be clear about that distinction yourself, and work at making it clear in the group study.

2. On the basis of your own study form a clear idea *before* the group meets of (i) the main theme(s) of the passage which should be opened out for discussion, and (ii) some general conclusions the group ought to reach as a result of the study. Here the questions which arise from 2 Timothy 3:16–17 should act as our guide.

3. The guidelines and questions which follow may help to provide a general framework for each discussion; leaders should use them as starting places which can be further developed. It is usually helpful to have a specific goal or theme in mind for group discussion, and one is suggested for each study. But even more important than tracing a single theme is understanding the teaching and the implications of the passage.

Leading the Group:

1. Announce the passage and theme for the study, and begin with prayer. In group studies it may be helpful to invite a different person to lead in prayer each time you meet.

2. Introduce the passage and theme, briefly reminding people of its outline and highlighting the content of each subsidiary section.

3. Lead the group through the discussion questions. Use your own if you are comfortable in doing so; those provided may be used, developing them with your own points. As discussion proceeds, continue to encourage the group first of all to discuss the significance of the passage (teaching) and only then its application (meaning for us). It may be helpful to write important points and applications on a board by way of summary as well as visual aid.

4. At the end of each meeting, remind members of the group of their assignments for the next meeting, and encourage them to come prepared. Be sufficiently prepared as the leader to give specific assignments to individuals, or even couples, or groups, to come with specific contributions.

5. Remember that you are the leader of the group! Encourage clear contributions, and do not be embarrassed to ask someone to explain what they have said more fully or to help them to do so ('Do you mean … ?').

Most groups include the 'over-talkative', the 'over-silent' and the 'red-herring raisers'! Leaders must control the first, encourage the second and redirect the third! Each leader will develop his or her own most natural way of doing that; but it will be helpful to think out what that is before the occasion arises! The first two groups can be helped by some judicious direction of questions to specific individuals or even groups (for example, 'Jane, you know something about this from personal experience …'); the third by redirecting the discussion to the passage itself ('That is an interesting point, but isn't it true that this passage really concentrates on… ?'). It may be helpful to break the group up into smaller groups sometimes, giving each subgroup specific points to discuss and to report back on. A wise arranging of these smaller groups may also help each member to participate.

More important than any techniques we may develop is the help of the Spirit enabling us to understand and to apply the Scriptures. Have and encourage a humble, prayerful spirit.

6. Keep faith with the schedule; it is better that some of the group wished the study could have been longer than that others are inconvenienced by it stretching beyond the set time limits.

7. Close in prayer. As time permits, spend the closing minutes in corporate prayer, encouraging the group to apply what they have learned in praise and thanks, intercession and petition.

COLOSSIANS

STUDY 1: COLOSSIANS 1:1-8

AIM: To begin to grasp why Paul is writing this letter to the church in Colossae and to see where his confidence lies about its being well received by the Christians there.

1. As Paul introduces himself in the opening verse of the letter, what do we learn about him personally, especially in terms of his authority to write to the church in this way? (1:1)

2. In keeping with the accepted style of letter-writing of his day the apostle identifies the people to whom this letter is addressed (1:2). What do we learn from the tone, content and his form of greeting in this verse? Why, especially, does Paul refer to these believers as being 'in Christ'?

3. It was almost invariably Paul's custom in his letters to include a reference to his prayers for those to whom he is writing and that is what he does here. Given that the reason behind this letter is to address problems in the church, why does he begin on a note of thankfulness? (1:3)

4. What two things in particular does Paul point to as being the reason for his always thanking God for the church in Colossae and why are they important? (1:3-5)

5. Paul speaks of 'the hope laid up for you in heaven' that lies behind these people's faith in Christ and love for all the saints.

How does he go on to explain this hope more fully and show why it lies at the heart of true Christian experience? (1:5-6)

6. What does this teach us about the kind of evidence we ought to see in someone's life which shows that they really are a Christian?

7. Why does Paul mention Epaphras at the end of this section? (1:7, 8) If a trusted friend were to bring a report about you or your church to someone else, what do you think they would say?

STUDY 2: COLOSSIANS 1:9-14

AIM: To explore the prayer that Paul offers for his readers at the beginning of his letter to see how it discreetly identifies the key issues the Colossian Christians are struggling with in their church and maps out the main things Paul wants them to learn from his letter.

1. Having already told these Christians that he and his companions always thank God for the church in Colossae, Paul now tells them they also continuously pray for them (1:9). What does that say about Paul as a pastor, given the busyness of his life, and what does it say to us about our concern for our fellow Christians?

2. What is the first thing Paul asks God to give these Christians and how do you think God would provide what he is requesting? (1:9)

3. It would be tempting to see 'being filled with the knowledge of his will in all spiritual wisdom and understanding' as a very private and personal thing. How does Paul make it clear that it is actually something with a very public face? (1:10)

4. What do we learn, about ourselves as much as about the Colossians, from the fact that Paul uses present continuous tenses in this verse?

5. Where does Paul say that the strength not just to live the Christian life, but to keep on going comes from? (1:11)

6. Why is it significant that Paul refers to 'patience', 'joy' and thankfulness as he prays for this church's progress in the life of faith? (1:11-12)

7. How is what God has promised in the future for his people linked to what he has done in the past through his Son? (1:12-13) What difference should that make as we try to live as Christians?

8. What does Paul mean by the word 'redemption' and why is it so important to the way we understand what it means to be a Christian? (1:14)

STUDY 3: COLOSSIANS 1:15-23

AIM: To begin to appreciate what it means for Jesus to be Lord of all creation and head of the church and to see how that undergirds our self-understanding as Christians in terms of who we are and how we now live through our relationship with him.

1. How would the Colossians' view of Jesus Christ be altered through knowing he is 'the image of the invisible God' and 'the firstborn of all creation? (1:15) How does this affect the way we view the world we live in on the one hand, and Jesus on the other?

2. Bearing in mind the ideas about the unseen world of spiritual powers that were creeping into the situation in Colossae, why does Paul go on to emphasize Christ's authority over the invisible as well as the visible realm of creation? (1:16)

3. How does the statement about Christ that 'he is before all things and in him all things hold together' (1:17) reinforce what Paul has been saying in the previous two verses? How might people – both Christian and non-Christian – react to that assertion today?

4. How does Paul describe what Jesus is in relation to his church? (1:18) Was this the way he was understood by the Colossians and is this how he is regarded by the average Christian today?

5. What light does Paul shed on the greatness of the salvation promised in the gospel through what he says here about the Person of Christ and the work he accomplished on the cross? (1:19-20)

6. As Paul spells out what the finished work of Christ meant for the Colossians, what difference has this made to them and what is the ultimate goal to which it will finally lead? (1:21-22) Why is it so important for every Christian to keep these two things in mind?

7. Why does Paul qualify what he has just stated by saying 'if indeed you continue in the faith' and why does he link this specifically to 'the gospel that you heard' on the one hand and the fact that he was a 'minister' of that gospel on the other? (1:23)

STUDY 4: COLOSSIANS 1:24-2:5

AIM: To see how Paul explains what is involved in the ministry he had been given and the struggles it entailed and shows how his sufferings in that ministry only make sense in light of the genuineness of the gospel he was called to preach.

1. How can Paul say that he 'rejoices' in his sufferings and what does he mean when he says that in his flesh he is 'filling up what is lacking in Christ's affliction for the sake of his body'? (1:24-25) Was this true only for Paul in a special sense, or does it continue to be true for every Christian who seeks to faithfully communicate the gospel?

2. Why does Paul describe the message of the gospel as 'the mystery hidden for ages and generations but now revealed to his saints'? (1:26) Why is this different from saying that the gospel is something mystical?

3. What was it specifically that Paul says God had chosen to make known to his saints? (1:27) What does this say about the depth of

relationship a Christian has with God through their union with Christ in salvation? How does this alter our outlook on our present circumstances and our future hope if we are believers?

4. How are we to understand the way he puts 'I toil' and 'he [God] powerfully works' side by side in this verse? (1:28) Look up Philippians 2:12-13: in what ways does this help us to see that what was true for Paul is also true for every Christian?

5. Why is Paul so anxious that his readers should be aware of the struggle he has been experiencing in the work of the ministry? (2:1-2) How might this lead to their hearts being 'encouraged'?

6. What is the goal the apostle is aiming for as he labours at such personal cost in his efforts to teach the gospel to these people? (2:2-3)

7. What is Paul anxious to guard his readers against? (2:4) In what way do Christians and churches still need this kind of protection today and how will they find it?

8. Even though Paul is not physically present with the Christians in Colossae, how can he say that he is 'rejoicing to see your good order and the firmness of your faith in Christ'? (2:5) How should that affect the way we relate and react to what God is doing in the lives of his people in other parts of the country and of the world?

STUDY 5: COLOSSIANS 2:6-15

AIM: To see that if people have received Christ Jesus as Lord, their new life in relationship with him must work itself out in a whole new way of life as they begin to live in fellowship with him.

1. What is the basic principle of the Christian life that Paul is setting out in this verse? (2:6) How should this colour our outlook on everyday life if we are Christians?

2. Paul mixes metaphors in what he goes on to say about 'roots' and buildings (2:6-7). What is he teaching about the link between the hidden and visible aspects of the life of faith? Why does he include in this the reference to 'abounding in thanksgiving'?

3. What two dangers does Paul tell the Colossians to guard themselves against and what two spheres do they come from? (2:8) How can they make sure they are not misled in these ways?

4. How does what Paul goes on to say about the uniqueness of Christ, as he is set forth in the gospel, provide the ultimate safeguard against people being misled in their search for salvation? (2:9, 10) What does this say about how central Christ must be in the teaching and worship of the church in all ages?

5. Looking at the structure of the one sentence that spans these two verses, in what way do the rites of circumcision and baptism find the focus of what they both symbolize in Christ? (2:11-12) How does this help us to understand the connection between circumcision in the Old Testament and baptism in the New?

6. How does Paul go on to show that it is not by rites and ceremonies in themselves that God changes people's lives, but through the One to whom these rituals point? (2:13-14) Why is the cross of Christ central to what Paul is saying here?

7. What is the connection between what Paul has just been saying about the cross and spiritual 'rulers and authorities' being 'put to open shame'? (2:15) How was that intended to be an encouragement to the Colossian Christians and in what way is it an encouragement to us today?

STUDY 6: COLOSSIANS 2:16-19

AIM: To see that in the church in Colossae as much as in the church of all ages, it is not outward traditions and religious regulations that lead to spiritual growth and progress, but rich and deep communion with God through Jesus Christ.

1. What kind of outward regulations were being imposed upon the Christians in Colossae as the key to making progress in the Christian life? (2:16) In what ways might Christians today be put under similar pressure?

2. Why were such things of no value when it came to bringing about the kind of spiritual progress that was being claimed for them? (2:17) Why, then, have such things always seemed appealing, even to those who are sincere in the faith?

3. As Paul highlights the contrast between what he calls 'shadow' and 'substance', how does he help his readers where the key to spiritual life and vitality is to be found and why? (2:17) In what ways might we reverse the order of that contrast and allow Christ to become too 'shadowy' in our thinking?

4. Paul goes on to point to an unnamed individual who was evidently known to his readers and who was effectively holding them to ransom through what he was teaching (2:18) How does Paul respond to the influence he was exerting? Think of similar ways in which people in churches you have known might exert the same kind of influence.

5. Where was the fundamental flaw in what this person was teaching that was the telltale sign that he had drifted from the apostolic gospel? (2:19)

6. How does Paul then focus on what was so critically absent in the kind of teaching that was taking hold in Colossae to show that it is actually what needs to be crucially central to the life of faith? (2:19) Look up Ephesians 4:15-16: How does Paul's teaching in this parallel passage help to flesh out what he is saying to the Colossians?

STUDY 7: COLOSSIANS 2:20-23

AIM: To understand that being united with Christ in his death has profound implications for how we understand ourselves as Christians and the kind of things we allow ourselves to be controlled by in the Christian life.

1. What does Paul mean when he describes a Christian as someone who 'with Christ...died to the elemental spirits of the world? (2:20) – Look back at Colossians 2:8 to see what Paul says about 'elemental spirits' there.

2. Look up Romans 6:1-7: How do these verses throw additional light on what Paul is teaching in this part of Colossians – especially in terms of our no longer being 'enslaved to sin' (*Rom.* 6:6-7)? What practical difference should that make to the way we face temptation as Christians?

3. How does Paul apply this principle to the Colossians and the kind of things that were controlling their lives? (2:20-21)

4. The apostle goes on to explain what makes the regulations that were being imposed on the Christians in Colossae false (2:22). How does this clarification help us to see the distinction between religious rules that have no place in the life of the church and those that do and should?

5. Why is it that rules that involve 'asceticism and severity to the body' have 'the appearance of wisdom' and not only were appealing to the believers in Colosse, but have had an enduring appeal to Christians through the centuries? (2:23)

6. Why are the kinds of things Paul has been describing 'of no value in stopping the indulgence of the flesh'? (2:23) How does this tie in with what he has been saying about the centrality of the cross and all that Jesus accomplished there for his people in dealing with the power of sin as well as with its consequences?

STUDY 8: COLOSSIANS 3:1-4

AIM: To grasp something of the far-reaching significance of Christ's resurrection – in particular in terms of its impact on the new life we have as Christians and the ability it gives us to live no longer for ourselves and for this world, but for God.

1. Paul reminds the Colossians that when they became Christians they were 'raised with Christ' (3:1). Since that was true, what difference should that make to the kind of things they 'seek', or 'set their hearts on' in life?

2. What sort of things are we so often inclined to set our hearts on even as Christians and, as we think about specific examples, what does that teach us about ourselves and what really matters to us? Look up Matthew 6:19-21: How does this help us to appreciate more fully what Paul is teaching here?

3. How does the full weight of this teaching become more apparent as Paul speaks about seeking not merely 'things that are above', but the fact that this is 'where Christ is, seated at the right hand of God?'

4. What is different between what Paul says in the first verse and what he says in the second? (3:2) What does this tell us about the importance of our minds and the way we use them in the Christian life? What difference might this make to how much we are expected to use our minds when we gather as the church to worship God?

5. Why does Paul reinforce what he is saying in these opening verses in this chapter with the negative injunction 'and not on things that are on earth'? (3:2) What kind of earthly things loom too large on the horizons of our lives and become a distraction to our faith? What kind of religious things fall into this category?

6. What does Paul mean when he says, 'For you have died and your life is hidden together with Christ in God'? (3:3) How does that provide comfort and encouragement for Christians?

7. How are we to interpret Paul's qualifying comment about Christ when he says, 'who is your life'? (3:4) What light does this throw on the depth of our relationship with Christ and how should that affect us in practical terms?

8. How should the promise about Christ's return in glory that Paul spells out here help us to see where our focus in life needs to be fixed? (3:4)

STUDY 9: COLOSSIANS 3:5-11

AIM: To see how Paul develops and applies his teaching about the Christian's union with Christ in his death and resurrection in terms of how we deal with sin in our lives.

1. Why is the word 'therefore' so important to our understanding of what Paul is saying at the beginning of this new section? (3:5) What does it tell us about where we find the resources we need to deal with sin, not just in some cosmetic sense, but at its very roots in our lives?

2. What kind of sins does Paul specifically identify in this verse? (3:5) What makes them so subtle and yet so dangerous? What is involved in 'putting sin to death'?

3. For many Christians the one thing that prevents them from getting caught up in some of the sins mentioned here is the fear of being caught. What does Paul point to as the most compelling reason to avoid such things? (3:6) Why do you think the concept of the 'wrath of God' is treated so lightly as much by Christians as by the secular world in our day?

4. Why does Paul remind these Colossian Christians of what they used to be prior to their conversion? (3:7). How does remembering what we have been rescued from help us to gain a deeper appreciation of Christ and what he means to us each day?

5. What kind of sins does Paul specifically identify in this verse? (3:8) What makes them so subtle and yet so dangerous? What is involved in 'putting these sins away'?

6. Over against the negative injunctions Paul has been issuing in these verses, what is the great positive reason he provides as to why and how they should be fulfilled? (3:9-10) What should this mean in terms of trust and transparency in the life of God's family?

7. What can we learn from Paul's reminder that, as Christians, we 'have put on the new self which is being renewed in knowledge after the image of its creator'? (3:10)

8. How does the final verse in this section tie in to all that Paul has been saying in it – primarily in relation to what was happening in Colossae, but also in the life of the church generally? (3:11)

STUDY 10: COLOSSIANS 3:12-17

AIM: To appreciate the positive dimension of what it means to cultivate a life of holiness as Christians, not just in what we are and do privately and personally, but together as the family of God in the church.

1. How does the word 'then' (3:12) link this passage not only with the one that immediately precedes it (3:5-11), but also the larger section of which it is a part (2:20-3:4)? In what way does this help us to see the two sides of growing in holiness?

2. Why does Paul introduce this section by reminding the Colossian Christians that they are 'God's chosen ones, holy and beloved' (3:12)? Why is it important for us as Christians to understand who we are in Christ before we try to live for him?

3. What do the qualities Paul lists in these verses as things the Christians should 'put on' or 'clothe' themselves with, say about the way holiness affects our relationships? (3:12-13)

4. Why does Paul say, 'Above all these things put on love' (3:14)? How does this point us to God who 'is love' (*1 John* 4:8) on the one hand and for human beings to be made in his image and likeness on the other (*Gen.* 1:26)?

5. When Paul says 'And let the peace of Christ rule in your hearts' (3:15), what would that have meant for the Colossians as they were 'called in the one body' and what does it mean for us as Christians today?

6. How does Paul show that receiving and benefiting from 'the word of Christ' is never merely something private and personal, but something that affects how we minister to others? (3:16)

7. What does it mean to 'do everything in the name of the Lord Jesus'? (3:17)

8. Why does Paul stress the importance of being 'thankful' and 'giving thanks to God' three times in the space of three verses? (3:15-17) What does that say about the spirit in which we ought to live our lives as Christians?

STUDY 11: COLOSSIANS 3:18-4:1

AIM: To appreciate how holiness – being set apart from the world for the Lord – makes a difference not just to what we are and how we live in our lives individually, but must also transform the way we relate to all kinds of people.

1. Paul singles out three sets of relationships in these verses: wives and husbands, children and fathers, slaves and masters (3:18-4:1). Why do you think he chose these relationships in particular?

2. The idea of wives 'submitting' to their husbands is hardly popular (3:1). What are some of the wrong perceptions of submission that make people recoil from this teaching? Looking closely

at how Paul presents it, how does he show it is something which is genuinely good and beneficial?

3. What exhortation does the apostle give to husbands in relation to their wives? (3:19) Why do husbands need to be reminded of this throughout their married life and not just on their wedding day?

4. Ideas about parenting and how to bring up children are often thought to be culture-bound. How do the instructions Paul gives to both children and their fathers (and, by extension, to their mothers) rise above the level of mere cultural norms? (3:20-21)

5. Why were Paul's instructions to slaves and their masters so counter-cultural in the time in which Paul was writing? (3:22-4:1). How can the principles contained in these instructions be applied in the days in which we live?

6. Why do you think it is significant that, in all three sets of relationships that Paul addresses here, he relates the way Christians relate to other people to how they relate to the Lord? (3:18, 20, 22, 24)

7. Speaking to slave masters, Paul reminds them on the one hand that there is accountability for wrong-doing (3:25) and on the other that they 'also have a Master in heaven' (4:1). What did this say to these slave owners in particular and what does it say to us?

STUDY 12: COLOSSIANS 4:2-6

AIM: To grasp the nature and importance of prayer in relation to how the gospel spreads and how that in turn must spill over into the kind of lives we live as Christians before a watching world.

1. How does what Paul says to the Colossians about their prayer life (4:2) echo what he has already told them about his own prayer life (1:3, 9) and what Luke says about the place of prayer in the

early church (*Acts* 2:42)? What does this teach us about the discipline of prayer for all believers?

2. What does it mean to be 'watchful' in prayer and to pray 'with thanksgiving'? (4:2)

3. What does it say about Paul and his companions that he asks for prayer for himself and his colleagues in the ministry? (4:3) Why is it too often the case that those involved in Christian work do not have the same sense of needing the prayers of others?

4. What are the specific things Paul asks the Colossians to remember in prayer as they intercede for him and for his work? (4:3-4) How might the same things affect the priorities we have in our own praying?

5. How does Paul say the Colossians ought to live before 'outsiders'? (4:5) What does this say to all Christians and the care they give to the way they live their lives before those around them who are not yet Christians?

6. Why does the apostle link this to the way they regard and use 'time'? (4:5) How does the broader view of 'time' and 'history' that the Bible gives us, especially in the New Testament, make a difference to how we use our time in the narrower sense?

7. What does Paul say about our speech as Christians and what do you think he means by this? (4:6) Where is this kind of speech meant to lead as we converse with those who have questions about the Christian faith?

STUDY 13: COLOSSIANS 4:7-18

AIM: To realize that this closing section in Paul's letter is more than just a random list of friends and acquaintances that Paul chooses to mention, but rather an integral part of all he has been teaching – showing that they too reflect the kind of life he has been describing in the body of the letter.

1. Why is Paul sending Tychicus and Onesimus to visit the Christians in Colossae? (4:7-9) How does the language he uses to describe them set the Colossians at ease as they anticipate their arrival? What does this say to us about the importance of encouraging fellow Christians – even in far-off places – who may be discouraged?

2. What particular flavour would each of the greetings from Aristarchus, Mark and Jesus called Justus have conveyed to the Colossian church? (4:10-11) How should that help us to appreciate the unique contribution that every believer can make to the fellowship of the church?

3. Why would Paul's comments about Epaphras have made a special impact on his audience in Colossae? (4:12-13) What in particular would have struck them about the way he prayed, what he prayed for and the fact that it was consistent with the wider work he was doing in the church?

4. The next three names Paul includes may seem quite disconnected, but what does he convey by placing them side by side? (4:14-15) What does Paul's awareness of so many other people in the wider church say about his concern for the family of God? In what ways might we become too parochial in our view of the church?

5. Why do you think the apostle was eager to ensure that the letters he wrote to different churches were circulated to other churches? (4:16) How does this help to guard against a very insular attitude to church life and what it means to be a Christian?

6. How might the seemingly throwaway remark about Archippus say something not only to this man himself, but to the need for all Christians to be faithful in the calling God has given them and their commitment to the faith? (4:17)

7. In what ways do Paul's personal remarks in the closing verse tie together all he has been saying from the very start of the letter

as a whole? (4:18) How do they help us to gain a better appreciation of Paul the man?

8. If you were to identify just one thing from what you have learned in your study of Colossians, what would it be?

PHILEMON

STUDY 1: PHILEMON 1-25

AIM: To understand and appreciate the weight of Paul's request to Philemon and see how through it God has something vital to teach the church through all ages.

1. Take a few moments to read through this short letter, then think about and discuss the things that make it seem remote from the world we live in and the kind of issues Christians face today.

2. Why do you think Paul introduces himself to Philemon in the way he does (*Philem.* 1) in contrast to the way he introduced himself at the beginning of Colossians? How, then, does he go on to address Philemon and the other people he mentions? (*Philem.* 1-2) What does this teach us about the link between what we say and how we say it in our dealings with other people? In view of what Paul goes on to say in the rest of letter, why is his greeting especially appropriate? (*Philem.* 3)

3. What is significant about the things for which Paul gives thanks in relation to Philemon? (*Philem.* 4-5) How does this strengthen the case he is beginning to make for Onesimus' return to his owner? What specifically does he pray for in terms of Philemon's faith and its impact? (*Philem.* 6) Why is it important for Christians everywhere to grasp this principle? What can we learn from the personal testimony Paul adds to what he has been saying? (*Philem.* 7)

4. How does Paul seek to persuade Philemon to not only listen to, but respond to the request he is about to make? (*Philem.* 8-9) What does this teach us about the deepest motivation to right behaviour in the Christian life? In what way would Paul's description of what had happened to Onesimus help Philemon to see that God had genuinely worked in his life? (*Philem.* 10-12)

5. What do we learn regarding Onesimus from Paul's comments about how much he meant to him in prison? (*Philem.* 13) How did this in turn affect the way Paul approached Philemon on his behalf? (*Philem.* 14) In what way does Paul encourage Philemon to view Onesimus and his actions, not merely from a human point of view, but in light of what God had been doing through it all? (*Philem.* 15-16) Why is it important for us as Christians to always keep that perspective in mind as we try to make sense of things that go wrong in life?

6. What is the big request that Paul makes of Philemon and why is it so challenging? (*Philem.* 17) How does Paul demonstrate the sincerity and seriousness of what he is asking? (*Philem.* 18-19) In what way is this reinforced by what he says about 'benefit' and being 'refreshed in heart' through Philemon's response? (*Philem.* 20) How does this change how we see our behaviour and the fact it often has more far-reaching impact than we realize?

7. How can Paul be so sure that Philemon will not only respond positively to his request but actually exceed his expectations? (*Philem.* 21) How does this show itself as Paul makes plans for the future and what does all this say about the way our confidence in one another as members of God's family grows and proves itself in action? (*Philem.* 22)

8. The greetings at the end of Paul's letters can sometimes feel irrelevant to us as readers who do not know the people from whom they come. How does the inclusion of such greetings in a letter like this help us to see what true Christian fellowship looks like? (*Philem.* 23-24) Why does Paul's choice of words for the benediction form a fitting conclusion to this letter as a whole? (*Philem.* 25)

9. How would you sum up the main teaching of this letter in terms of its ongoing relevance to Christians through the ages and to you and your church today?

FOR FURTHER READING

J. PHILIP ARTHUR, *Christ All Sufficient* (Darlington: Evangelical Press, 2007).

MICHAEL BENTLEY, *The Guide: Colossians and Philemon* (Darlington: Evangelical Press, 2002).

F. F. BRUCE, *The Epistles to the Colossians, and to Philemon* (Grand Rapids, MI: Eerdmans, 1984).

HERBERT M. CARSON, *Colossians and Philemon* (Leicester: IVP, 1983).

JOHN DAVENANT, *Colossians* (1627, repr. Edinburgh: Banner of Truth, 2005).

D. E. GARLAND, *Colossians/Philemon* (Grand Rapids, MI: Zondervan, 1998).

WILLIAM HENDRIKSEN, *Philippians, Colossians & Philemon*, (Edinburgh: Banner of Truth, 1962, repr. 1988).

R. KENT HUGHES, *Colossians and Philemon: The Supremacy of Christ* (Westchester IL: Crossway, 1987).

J. B. LIGHTFOOT, *Saint Paul's Epistles to the Colossians and to Philemon* (Westchester IL: Crossway, 1997).

DICK LUCAS, *The Message of Colossians and Philemon* (Leicester: IVP, 2000).

IAN MCNAUGHTON, *Opening up Colossians and Philemon* (Leominster: Day One Publications, 2007)

DOUGLAS J. MOO, *The Letters to the Colossians and to Philemon* (Nottingham: Apollos, 2008).

P. T. O'BRIEN, *Colossians-Philemon* (Waco, TX: Word Books, 1987).

R. W. WALL, *Colossians and Philemon* (Nottingham: IVP, 2010).

GEOFFREY B. WILSON, *New Testament Commentaries, Volume 2*, (Edinburgh: Banner of Truth, 2005).

ALSO AVAILABLE FROM
THE BANNER OF TRUTH

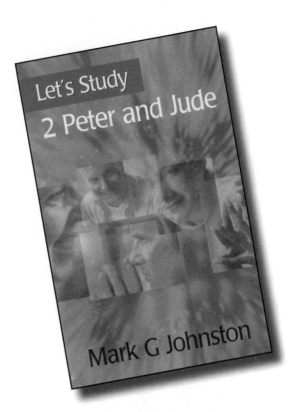

Let's Study 2 Peter & Jude
Mark Johnston

B oth Peter and Jude show that the problem of false doctrine is
nothing new among the people of God. By using examples from
the Old Testament, they encourage their fellow believers to remain
faithful to the gospel. Mark Johnston's contemporary commentary
shows that the themes which appear in 2 Peter and Jude are as rel-
evant for Christians today as they were in the first century.

> 'This is a fine book and it is apparent from the outset that it has
> been written with a pastor's heart. Every page exhibits a clear desire
> that readers today should take to heart the message of these letters.'
> *Evangelical Times*

ISBN 978 0 85151 917 2 | paperback | 144 pp.

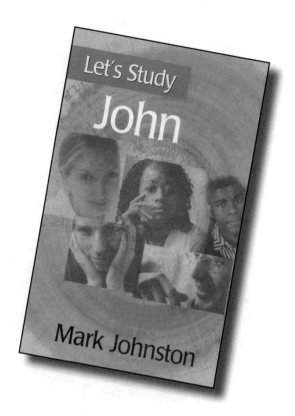

Let's Study John
Mark Johnston

Mark Johnston guides us through John's account of Jesus Christ, the Son of God. He shows that the Gospel of John can be seen as the reflective Gospel – a selection of the works and words of Christ for detailed contemplation. John takes us by the hand and leads us into the depths and mysteries of Christ's person and the wonders he has accomplished, so that the reader should come to living faith in Jesus as the Christ, the Son of God, and have eternal life in his name.

Another contemporary study guide from the expanding
Let's Study series, suitable for individual or group use.

ISBN 978 0 85151 833 6 | paperback | 320 pp.

Exposition of Colossians

John Davenant

Spurgeon considered this one of the best commentaries on Paul's letter to the Colossians. He approvingly quoted Charles Bridges' words about this volume: 'I know of no exposition upon a detached portion of Scripture (with the single exception of Owen on the Hebrews) that will compare with it in all parts... in depth, accuracy, and discursiveness.'

The Trust first reprinted this much praised commentary in 2005 with the hope that is would continue to instruct, encourage and sanctify the faith and life of Christian people in the 21st century.

ISBN 978 0 85151 909 8 | clothbound | 400 pp.

Philippians, Colossians & Philemon
William Hendriksen

W illiam Hendriksen's *New Testament Commentary*, of which this volume forms a part, was undoubtedly the foremost conservative and reformed commentary of the 20th century. The book contains a thorough introduction to each epistle, together with verse-by-verse comments – indeed it is so written that the needs of the advanced scholar, or the pastor, or the layman will be satisfied. This would be a worthwhile addition to any Christian's library.

ISBN 0 85151 455 3 | clothbound | 248 pp.

The Banner of Truth Trust originated in 1957 in London. The founders believed that much of the best literature of historic Christianity had been allowed to fall into oblivion and that, under God, its recovery could well lead not only to a strengthening of the church today but to true revival.

Inter-denominational in vision, this publishing work is now international, and our lists include a number of contemporary authors along with classics from the past. The translation of these books into many languages is encouraged.

A monthly magazine, *The Banner of Truth*, is also published and further information will be gladly supplied by either of the offices below or from our website.

THE BANNER OF TRUTH TRUST

3 Murrayfield Road
Edinburgh, EH12 6EL
UK

PO Box 621, Carlisle
Pennsylvania, 17013
USA

www.banneroftruth.co.uk